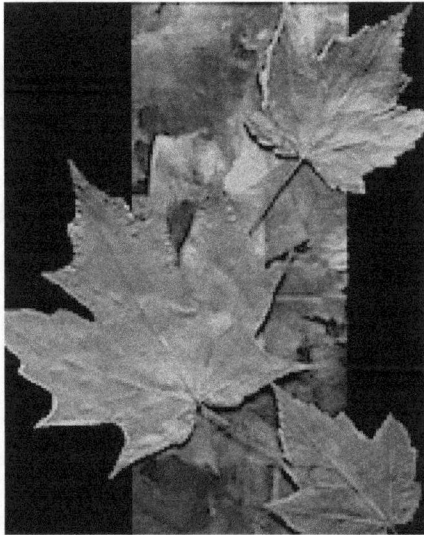

STRADDLING YOUR FREEDOM

by

Robert P. Theiss

Ancient Wings®
The Teachings of Michael

Products and Services

Books/Journals
Living Inside your Passion
Straddling your Freedom
Writing Journals – Gratitude Series

The Teachings of Michael
Friends of Spirit Program
Home Study Courses
Sessions with Spirit
Channel Library

Please Visit:
www.ancientwings.com

Straddling your Freedom
By Robert P. Theiss

Copyright © 2007 by Robert P.Theiss
First Edition – Riding a Stallion/Igniting the Fire
Second Edition – 2010; revised
ISBN 978-0-578-00664-2 (2007)
ISBN 978-0-578-06433-8 (2010)
Published by Ancient Wings
P.O. Box 1148
North Plains, Oregon 97133

The author of this book does not dispense medical advice or prescribe any technique as a form of treatment for physical or emotional problems and therefore assumes no responsibility for your actions.

The intent of this material is to provide general information to help your quest for emotional and spiritual growth. We encourage you to seek professional assistance for all areas of healing.

Design: Ancient Wings
Editorial supervision: Gena Duel
Cover images: Koka Filipovic
Interior chapter heading image: Koka Filipovic
Backcover photo: Shirley Collins

Printed in the United States of America

i

Straddling Your Freedom

About the Author

Robert Theiss openly shares a conscious relationship he has developed with Spirit, including the presence of Archangel Michael, Yeshua and Father Spirit. He is an internationally recognized artist, author and healer who teaches with compassion, humor and joy. His messages are always uplifting, self-empowering and based in love. He has served and shared the Teachings of Michael since 1998 and is the founder and director of Ancient Wings®.

For more information on the Teachings of Michael feel free to visit his website.

Ancient Wings

P.O. Box 1148

North Plains, Oregon 97133

(503) 858-5039

Email: info@ancientwings.com

www.ancientwings.com

Acknowledgments

There are so many friends and family who have contributed in their own way to making this book a reality. I would like to thank my wife for her unending support, her patience, and her willingness to help guide me back to my heart. To my first love, this Earth, your beauty will never be forgotten. I want to thank Géna for her editing and transcribing skills. Without your help, this book would not have been possible. To my dear friend Archangel Michael, thank you for guiding me back to my soul!

Contents

Chapter One

Igniting the Fire

It is a warm, spring day here in Oregon. The song of a robin keeps me company reminding me once again how nature so freely celebrates each moment. A bee passes my window and stops long enough just to say hello. A deer drinks from a nearby stream, unconcerned by the activities of our neighbors. Overhead, a hawk slowly circles the sky, perceiving life with an overview that scans the vast landscape below. On this day, I am preparing myself to once again share a relationship I have developed with Spirit, including the presence of Archangel Michael with another

1

group of people. I imagine sitting next to a tree, feeling its roots enter the warm, wet soil of the earth. I envision these roots descending all the way into the center of this planet. My body begins to feel a warm, soothing energy rising up through my feet as I maintain this imagined connection with the earth. Her presence serves to help me relax as I begin to now feel the presence of another energy coming into the top of my head. It is very intense, blazing with a passion that literally takes my breath away. These energies from above and below me merge at my heart and I experience a profound, ecstatic wave of bliss resonating in every cell of my body.

The energy in this moment is simply delicious. These ecstatic waves of love ignite my senses, reminding me of a reality that my heart has yearned to feel all my life. Even my mind is amazingly quiet. It is speechless. The presence of this energy seems to act as an elixir to all my doubts and concerns. All of my physical discomforts seem to just dissolve by simply relaxing into this energy.

In this moment I experience myself as being truly fulfilled. Could this be our natural state of consciousness? I believe that it is and have shifted my allegiance to make choices that will accommodate this energetic connection.

To feel loved by all of life with an undying devotion to first love ourselves.

I continue to relish this love wash of energy and become conscious of a stream of thoughts that are very different from my usual internal dialog. They share a wisdom filled with compassion for our human dilemma. My heart begins to stir, seeking to express itself, unfiltered by the parameters of my past. My mind begins to translate the thoughts into words as my heart and body now begin to blaze from the fire expressed within this energy.

Another deep breath, I slowly open my eyes and greet the group of people who have come to hear, feel, and learn how they too can bring this experience into their own life. Connected to this energy, the colors in my physical surroundings are intensely vibrant, fluid, and responsive. Objects around me seem to respond to my touch like a string on a guitar. My mind begins to translate this stream of consciousness into words, a message, or a story that is laced in love.

"Good evening! This lifetime for each of you offers a most profound opportunity to reunite the divided aspects of your own consciousness. This unification of yourself reawakens your natural state of being—love. It is our joy to serve this love by reminding you how you may receive this gift in your day-to-day reality. As you begin to reunite these aspects, your identity slowly accepts the support of a vast, nonphysical soul family.

"Each and every moment that you choose love for yourself, you strengthen the foundation for a reality on earth that honors all of life. We stand before each of you deeply respecting your devotion to this love that embraces self-fulfillment and joy. We serve you by igniting the passion within your heart to burn away the inertia that denies you the very elixir to heal your polarized reality. It begins with you, dear soul. Will you allow the very perfection of who you are at this moment to be loved?

"We are the Family of Michael! Sitting at the heart of this family is our beloved friend, Archangel Michael. We joyfully resonate as a group consciousness to the fire of creation. We are but one of many soul families that are here to assist you. We stand before each of you honoring your choice to be on earth at this time. You volunteered to participate in a reality where you would forget your lineage and demonstrate how a human being can reconnect with their spiritual roots. You have tasted the pain of humanity's separation. Now is the time to break the shackles that confined your own consciousness, and reveal the nature of love in human form."

Igniting the Fire

The session continues into the night. My singular, human nature expands with each breath to include this collective soul family consciousness. I naturally begin to address myself as 'we.' Within this nonphysical family there exists an overwhelming sense of respect and honor for our human journey—a time on earth that would be the most challenging and the most rewarding of all our lifetimes.

Several hours pass as another session comes to a close. Archangel Michael begins to slowly step back as we acknowledge each other as friends. Joining him, as always, is the energy of Yeshua. They invite me to relax and receive their gratitude for the work we do together. Our relationship is supported by my willingness to walk in both worlds. In this walk I take full responsibility for my own life and continue to learn how to integrate Spirit into my day-to-day reality. A reality that for most of us has been anything but fulfilling.

These are incredible times we live in. Spiritual teachings that were once reserved for only a few are now available to anyone. 'Ordinary' people from any walk of life can experience the presence and love from their soul family, as the etheric energy around earth has shifted, allowing for this divine communion. Our history is filled with the pain and struggle of humanity striving to feel loved. We have been taught that to receive such a love, we must demonstrate that we are first worthy of such a gift. The fallacy of such a belief weighs heavy upon our human history.

A dramatic shift in consciousness is stirring the hearts of millions of people worldwide. The veil that separated our human adventure from our angelic friends has thinned. The concept of channeling has become accepted by many, with the majority of people believing that angels do indeed exist. This book however is not about channeling or hoping that the angels will make our life more fulfilling. It is about embodying a state of consciousness that allows us to enjoy a more intimate and direct relationship with our physical and nonphysical friends.

In our separation, prayer was most often used to communicate our desires with Spirit, hoping someone up there was listening. Many are now experiencing a direct relationship with a love that exists within all of life. By learning to 'be in receivership,' nature, the elements, and our angelic family are able to share a love that is supportive and noninvasive. We are slowly moving away from a victimized relationship with life, hoping and praying that we deserve God's blessings by learning to receive and feel the continuous flow of love that life has always offered. We are becoming empowered. We are becoming sovereign. We are becoming Spirit also!

My relationship with the Family of Michael grew over several years. It did not demand of me to first become enlightened nor did it ask that I perfect myself before I was qualified to receive Michael's friendship. It simply asked of me to have an honest relationship with myself. To stop denying the energy I had felt since my childhood. That realization and the eventual experiences that followed have served to remind me that Spirit, unlike humanity, has no agenda. This has been such a refreshing concept, made all the more real by Michael's presence.

Translating the energy of this 'family' into words is much like listening to a concert. A solo performance can be very intimate and rewarding. The dynamics, however, of listening to an orchestra adds so many more intricate textures and flavors. In this relationship with the Family of Michael, my heart acts as the conductor with this orchestration of energies. Archangel Michael serves as the guest conductor as he weaves and blends this group consciousness into a 'thought package' that my mind translates into words. I do not hear voices in my head. Nor does Michael take over my body. In fact, he refused to participate when I tried to disown my part in this relationship. It is a mutual, shared experience that is available to anyone.

As a child, I would spend countless hours feeling and playing with this nonphysical family. Over time, my connection became diminished as I learned to adapt to my new physical environment and its expectations. Our devotion as children began to shift to our physical family, friends, classmates and community. We inherited their beliefs, conditions and parameters in order to be accepted, to be loved. Not all of us did that very gracefully, and many of us endured both physical and emotional abuses. It was not until I was a senior in high school, during the early 1970s, that my devotion shifted again.

There was a collective uprising at that time on the planet in response to the established restrictions of our creative expressions. The energy of these times supported the desire for an authentic experience with life. I quickly developed, like many others, an enormous appetite for spiritual knowledge. The teachings of Don Juan, as written by Carlos Castaneda, had a profound impact on me. I was fascinated by the beliefs of eastern religions and native American teachings. Meditation and yoga quickly became a part of my life. The air was thick with the anticipation of change. Sacred mushrooms, LSD, and marijuana became a regular diet for many as a means to reconnect with a reality we left as children. These times were ripe for change as millions responded with tremendous enthusiasm.

Like many of my peers, my newfound freedom inspired me to explore this land. My backpack became my home for the next couple of years as I hitchhiked north to the mountains of Montana and south to the desert plains of Arizona. My travels included people from all walks of life, including priests and shamans. Living so close to nature, I discovered my first love—Earth. Her beauty was simply overwhelming to me. I was greeted each morning by the song of a bird and each night the crickets would guide me into my dreams. I had no plan, no agenda, no place to go, and no schedule. I gave my undivided attention to nature's voice, feeling her strike something deep within my heart. I spent my days being mesmerized by rambling streams, ever-changing skylines and the community of life that lived within the forests. Nature seemed so alive, enticing me to awaken from the hypnotic trance of my conditioned past.

Although I traveled by myself, for the first time in my life I never felt alone. I found myself spending hours just lying on the ground. It felt as if the earth herself was healing my heart, restoring a perception of life that valued joy. Joy is something that is truly lacking in our social, political, and religious institutions. These institutions help to define our identity by demanding that the mind be responsible for our perception of reality relegating the heart to a second class status. Our minds have been inundated with information, details, and endless descriptions of life. Science, mathematics, and athletics predominate. Our creative abilities became stagnant as we separated ourselves from a river of energy that supports all of life. Humanity is just now beginning to allow our divine nature to act as our new foundation. This lifetime, for most of us, is about building and securing a strong foundation that will support an emerging culture that respects our divine mind and sacred heart as being Spirit.

During this time, I began to experience unexplainable alternate realities that I believe were a natural byproduct of my desire to experience something authentic or real. Synchronistic events seemed to blend into my life without any effort. And yet, as much as I enjoyed this newfound freedom, I could not make peace with another part of me that endured and adapted to the conditions and beliefs of my past. It was always lurking behind the scenes, doubting the wisdom of my new choices. The more I explored the boundaries of my own consciousness, the more devoted this identity became to use my past as a reality check. As a young man, I became very frustrated with this division within myself. Just when my enthusiasm was blossoming, another part responded by applying the brakes. I quickly realized I did not have the tools to work with this inner conflict.

Such is the nature of our life here on earth. So much of our time has been spent feeling frustrated with our inability to relate to this division and relying on our past to offer safe passage into a known future.

The next 15 years of my life were devoted to living and exploring an alternative lifestyle. I eventually got married and helped to raise three children while living in the Oregon coast range. Surrounded by nature and with many other like-minded individuals, I immersed myself in a simple and very rewarding way of life. I was offered an apprenticeship to learn the trade of woodworking. The next six years were spent building weaving looms with my neighbor. My passions however shifted, and I started my own business as an artist building furniture. My craft became nationally recognized, and I continue to enjoy my relationship with the wood and my evolving designs.

It was during this time that I discovered the Seth books as channeled by Jane Roberts. The notion that we create our own reality was both stimulating and disturbing.

11

The words and energy of Seth inspired me to explore the nature of my own reality. I practiced automatic writing and found I had a talent for this. I truly enjoyed my life at this time as a father, artist, and husband, but residing within my heart was this underlying feeling that I was not allowing myself to fully embrace and embody the nature of my soul. The roles I was playing, although very fulfilling, did not leave me much time or energy to explore my core self. I became more conscious of how my past had influenced my present choices. It was safe for my conditioned past to co-exist within the roles that I had created for myself.

In 1987, a spiritual event called the Harmonic Convergence seemed to collectively make a mess of everyone's lives. It also served a deeper purpose. It reawakened a profound, spiritual vision for earth. A call to reclaim our spiritual heritage by healing our past and allowing our soul nature to reveal itself. It was at this time that I was introduced to a spiritual teacher and friend.

He was a man who channeled for a consciousness called Jabar. There are many forms of channeling, but this man would literally leave his body while Jabar offered his teachings. Jabar would freely share his perspective of our galactic and human history. Over the next six months, I was deeply honored by their friendship and devotion to inspire my heart to trust my passion. They challenged me to re-claim my sovereign nature and a deeper joy for living. Conscious, co-creating is a very powerful and vulnerable stance to take as a human being. It asks of us to have an honest, direct, and sincere relationship with ourselves and to acknowledge all the ways we have been seduced to play the victim by relying and depending on others for accep-tance and love.

During this period in my relationship with Jabar, I was awakened early one morning by the sound of a family of ravens. Their communication was filled with human under-tones; bickering, undermining, and gossiping. They would spend the next week waking me up each morning to their nonstop chattering modeling the very nature of our own inner dialog. Shortly thereafter, Jabar asked if I enjoyed my time with the ravens. I admitted that I had heard it all be-fore in my own head and while listening to others. In time it could drive a person crazy. I spent the next several months reflecting on my life and developed a sincere desire to heal the wounds of my past.

One night while driving home through Eugene, I ex-perienced a profound sense of being interconnected with all of life. At one point, the world literally stopped. I felt phys-ically connected with everything around me. The road, the

the car, and buildings all felt like an extension of my self. They were rippling with an energy as if to say, "How do we serve you now?" I shifted my attention to people and noticed their movements were in slow motion. It was like watching a ballet. The ongoing activities of other people in that moment were absolutely perfect. I experienced for the first time a sense of oneness with all of life which left my body feeling ecstatic. I experienced a reality outside of duality. This experience left me speechless. The love I felt for myself and for all of life in that moment was overwhelming. Tears started to flow and I knew my present life did not resonate with this energy. I would do anything to have this relationship with life.

Within a few months, I left my marriage, learned to accept a part-time role with my children, and began a new life as a healer, spiritual teacher, and artisan. During this period, nature invited me on a daily basis to simply sit, be still, and feel my connection with the rhythms of the earth. It was here in the silence of my mind that I could trust the clarity of my new choices. In the turmoil of separating from my family, I learned to serve my new devotion by spending hours, some times days, simply 'being' with nature. My heart was opening to a new freedom!

Over the next five years, I taught over a thousand students the art of using 'energy medicine' as a Reiki master. During this period, I began to feel the presence of a non-physical energy or being working alongside me. It literally felt like someone was standing right next to me. If I did not look directly at its presence, I could see a dark, blue glow. It was an invitation that would later reveal itself.

In one of my workshops, I met a woman who would become my best friend, fellow teacher, co-parent, and wife. She is a woman who is very comfortable 'being' in her feminine energies, helping me to heal many of the wounds that I developed from compromising my own worth and personal values. She introduced me to the art of embracing our fears as a means for healing our past. She also encouraged me to explore a spiritual practice called Tantra, the art of lovemaking that invites the presence of grand, archetypical male and female energies into the sacredness of our sexual experience. This type of intimacy and trust is a rare gift. Blending and merging our energies with another person can trigger deep wounds. Most of humanity has developed etheric shields that serve to protect our heart. We are just now learning to reconnect with life in a way that allows us to respect the sovereign nature of each soul. We do that by disconnecting from old patterns that are based on manipulation, extraction, and control.

Tantra dramatically changed my life by offering a re-union between my divine male and female counterparts. This relationship invites our male nature, the mind, to serve our heart, the sacred feminine, and discover that your true love, your soul mate, was within you all the time. My wife and I began to co-teach workshops that blended Reiki with our experiences of Tantra. The trust that I developed from this connection with my wife opened my mind to accept a communion with a nonphysical friend.

Out of curiosity, I contacted two renowned psychics to inquire about this blue presence in my life. They both laughed and went on to introduce me to Archangel Michael. Michael, through these intuitives, offered to co-teach with me as a friend. I was exhilarated and dumbfounded by this offer. Why was an Archangel hanging out with me? A part of me did not feel qualified to co-teach with Michael. Despite my concerns, his presence was very, very seductive. My resistance began to slowly melt as I now had the tools to work with my past feelings.

In private, I started to channel for Michael. I believed that to serve him I needed to get myself out of the picture. So I attempted many times to leave my body only to feel his presence also leaving. He was very clear with me that he was offering to 'co-teach' by blending and merging his consciousness with my own. It took me a few more years to truly honor and respect what my soul had to offer in this relationship. This dynamic friend would not allow me to use channeling as another means for separating myself from my own magnificence.

The relationship dramatically shifted as I came to re-spect and love myself. Michael's presence was now everywhere. Our social invitations evolved into unexpected sessions. The encouragement I received from my wife was unfailing, but my mind questioned my sanity on a daily ba-sis for wanting to share this relationship with the general public. It continued to insist that I was risking my profes-sional reputation as an artist. My mind believed that the Family of Michael was some kind of corporate takeover. The love wash that I experienced every time I felt their presence confirmed that the only thing that is truly fulfill-ing is being fulfilled.

In 2003, we opened our house as a meeting place for monthly sessions. They were recorded on CDs, and all of our workshops now included this evolving relationship. An agreement was made between Michael and myself: we will co-teach anything that I was willing to experience first-hand. Our friendship would be based on a mutual respect for the sovereign nature of my soul. I take full responsibility for my own life and agreed to share this unique relationship with others. I believe now that 'channeling' has served its purpose by introducing the presence of Spirit into our physical reality. It is now time not only to embrace the energy but also to embody it, representing a new emerging identity that allows for the presence of a 'soul family consciousness.'

Within the pages of this book is an invitation to expand your sense of family that also includes your nonphysical counterparts. It has challenged my human nature to explore the wonders of physical reality while connected to my soul. Spirit comes to us when we walk away from the polarized, dualistic reality that supports the vast majority of humanity at this time. This book can serve and inspire you in making that choice. Spirit becomes real when you allow it to be your life.

The Heart and Mind of Creation, Spirit has returned to earth. I invite you, dear reader, to explore a new perception of reality that truly honors Spirit. That will return to you your innate, creative abilities to experience whatever your heart desires. All of us have compromised our latent abilities to accommodate a collective consciousness. It is now time to allow the reunion of our divine mind and sacred heart within our physical body. A reunion that will truly awaken your freedom. It is waiting for you to choose a life whose existence is not based on your past. The true nature of Spirit is all inclusive. It has no fear. Ignite your passion and embrace your creativity with joy! Now is the time to trust that it is safe to reveal the beauty of your own creative abilities. My own joy is to be of service to Spirit, and this book is but one way I have chosen to express that joy. Dear reader, there is a stallion waiting for you on the horizon of your life inviting you to leave the struggles of separation and finally enjoy the ride of your life. Climb on, and experience what was always yours to know and feel - you are and have always been Spirit also.

Blessings,
Robert Theiss

Chapter Two

In the Beginning

We are the Family of Michael, a collective of individual identities that resonate with the fire aspect of Spirit. Our dear friend, Archangel Michael resides at the heart of this family. He stands with sword at hand to honor the ever-changing and evolving nature of life itself. We offer ourselves as fellow teachers with our physical counterparts. We bring a fresh perspective to encourage our dear friends on earth to awaken from a dream that has separated our realities. This dream has separated you, dear reader, from your inherent birthright of knowing yourself as being Spi-

Spirit! Our words cannot give you that knowing, but they can inspire you to experience this truth for yourself. A truth of realizing that life will serve you in any manner that you desire.

Each of you is here on earth at this time to become conscious of how life is indeed serving you. You are awakening from a deep trance that now invites you to reconsider your choices. The choice we place before each of you is for you to fall deeply in love with YOU. It seems so innocent and yet it unravels the many layers that have denied you such a feeling for yourself. It has denied you the experience of your own magnificent nature. Indeed, to be Spirit also invites your soul to heal your wounded heart and to acknowledge the boundaries and shields of your belief that you do not deserve this love. The manner in which this book has been written is our service to you. We wish to entice your heart to feel how deeply life honors and respects your presence. Our relationship with humanity is rapidly changing. No longer must you feel our angelic presence comes from a distant, more refined location. You feel our energy and believe that we, your angelic family, must have been granted a direct link to Spirit. We come to remind you, dear soul, that it is we who serve YOU.

Many of you have discovered access to the very energy that supports your angelic family. Many of you have taken this to heart, devoting yourself to a life that now serves this connection. You have discovered that the majority of humanity feels disconnected. This is challenging your conviction to share the same environment while perceiving a different reality. Not an easy task. In part, our energetic presence can reassure you that your sense of family and support need not be limited to your biological origins. As each of you becomes more conscious of how life wants to serve you, our relationship becomes more tangible and less dependent on your hopes, prayers, and faith.

Humanity continues to grow frustrated by the seemingly insurmountable problems that all of you face. However, there are a small number of humans who have discovered that the solutions to your collective conflicts reside within. These conflicts have not come from outside of your soul nature. The root cause can be traced to the very relationship you have with all aspects of your soul. Many of you are choosing to embrace a more cooperative, compassionate and sincere relationship with those aspects that feel polarized. That simple yet profound choice impacts all of life around you. We have the advantage of being able to perceive the energetic patterns that influence life on earth. Your planet is undergoing the most dramatic shift that has ever been witnessed in all of creation. You are experiencing Christ consciousness descending into every cell of your body. This consciousness knows itself to be Spirit. It recognizes itself as being All That Is. As it enters your life, dear soul, it recognizes a simple truth. I Am That I Am. At the core of all that you believe yourself to be lies this very presence, waiting for you to reclaim the inherent beauty of your own magnificence.

We, your nonphysical counterparts, have been celebrating now for some time. We see your hearts opening to allow your true nature to take residence within your body. Each one of you embodies the solution to your own conflicts. You are the ambassadors for Spirit itself. None of you are required to confront or oppose the consciousness that supports the majority of humanity at this time. There is a part of you that still loves to play that game. Christ consciousness has no agenda, as it knows itself to be whole within itself. Its love for self continuously seeks to expand its own sense of self. We are here to remind you that your service to this love is the very elixir to your planet's dilemma. Self-love, self-fulfillment, and self-nurturing supports a sovereign soul that is so filled with the essence of Spirit that it serves life with the overflow of love itself.

Your understanding of the nature of love is radically shifting away from self-sacrifice, compromise, and endless negotiations. You are moving from a victimized relationship with life to one of self-empowerment. You are becoming grand, conscious co-creators.

We come a bit closer to each of you as you are reading these pages to serve your trust that our presence and our love is real. As you heal the heart that has experienced love being withheld, you heal the belief that it is not safe to feel love in this physical environment. This leaves you feeling so vulnerable, trusting in something that is experienced by so few. This love we are speaking of is undeniable if you will but allow yourself to open up and receive it. Such is a trust that would have you drop your shields. These shields have served your fears for such a long time, maintaining a distant relationship with Spirit.

We are truly honored to witness the unfolding of a new understanding of how, in this new energy, love makes itself available to all of you. And we think you will agree that the timing could not have been better. Many of you recognize these times of change. It is a time to end the polarized relationship with life that begins within yourself by loving all aspects of your being. It is a time indeed that invites you to reclaim the glory and magnificence of your

24

own consciousness. Very few have tasted that freedom in your past. All of your religions are based on those individuals that allowed for this love that supports us to also support them, but never before has a group of human souls opened themselves to collectively embody a non-dualistic relationship with life.

Spirit was not always aware of itself, as it knows itself to be in this moment. We would like to take this moment then to share our perception of why you are here at this time on earth, why you are immersed, surrounded by a reality that seems to have forgotten the virtues of love. Take a deep breath and allow yourself to feel the support of a family consciousness that shares tremendous compassion and joy with you. Your understanding of God is changing, allowing for an experience that will challenge all of your definitions of Spirit.

Spirit Falls in Love

Imagine Spirit, spending eons of time in a place of introspection and absolute stillness. Some have tapped into this experience by creating that silence within themselves. In this state of being, a question occurred to Spirit, "What would my reality be like if I could perceive a reflection of my own self?" The magnitude of such a thought created a division within Spirit. The mind of Spirit, its male nature, was suddenly perceiving its female counterpart, the Heart of Creation. As Spirit gazed for the first time at its own reflection, something remarkable occurred. Spirit fell absolutely in love with itself. The mind of Spirit perceived the Heart of Creation to be its soul mate. The female nature of Spirit perceived the mind as being the most magnificent being in all of creation. Spirit was in love! Indeed, Spirit was in love with itself.

Spirit became so emphatically in love with its own reflection that it joyfully embraced itself. The male and female reached out to each other and embraced as lovers reunited. That embracement, that affection, ignited sparks of fire within Spirit. These sparks gave birth to multiple reflections of Spirit's love for itself. These reflections became known as the children of God, the Christed ones, or Christ consciousness. It was the birthing of individual and multiple aspects of Spirit. The children were supported and loved as one within a womb, an environment that became known as the kingdom. This environment supported this family of Spirit in a continuous bathing of love. Spirit's love for itself unleashed an experience of divine self-fulfillment.

Within this kingdom, all of life was united. There was never any sense of separation. Love was equally shared between all aspects within this united consciousness as it radiated from Spirit's love for itself. Fear and all of its attributes was unknown for it was never experienced. If you pause for a moment, you can feel the truth of this place by feeling the source of the yearning in your own heart to return to the kingdom. Here on earth, you sometimes feel it was all a dream. But it is not your imagination; the kingdom was your home. Your human experience is filled with memories of this place that are triggered by ecstatic moments of bliss and moments of great sadness.

Eons of time passed within this reality. It was a continuous love bath. Spirit, however, was contemplating the nature of love itself. The nature of freedom. Such a thought sparked other creative streams of thought offering the very gift of creation to all of its children.

Love Uncontained

Spirit contemplated a love that was not contained. A love without boundaries, a love that continuously expressed itself through all of the Christed ones. Unlimited freedom.

This thought brought tears of joy to Spirit. Granting this freedom to all of their children, Spirit could know itself

27

through the eyes of multiple, unlimited and sovereign reflections. Giving their own children free will to co-create
gave birth to the soul. A soul would embody all of Spirit's
attributes, fueled by a love for its own reflection. An individual soul would have complete freedom to use its
creative abilities ensuring that life would be eternal. A
freedom that would invite each soul to venture into unknown realities outside the safe boundaries of the kingdom.

And so Spirit addressed the Christed ones, offering
the gift to be a soul. A grand ceremony took place to honor
those who accepted this new identity. In time, these souls
were asked: "Who among you would like to venture into
unknown realities serving this love? Who among you
would like to be of service to this love outside the contained parameters of this kingdom, your home?"

Who did volunteer? It was the most adventurous within the kingdom, having never experienced anything but
love, who volunteered. This group of souls contemplated
this request with such affection for their Mother/Father.
They felt so loved, so adored, and so blessed that the gift of
creation would be bestowed upon them. They were deeply
honored and willingly raised their hands proclaiming: "We
will leave the kingdom to serve this love exploring and co-
creating into infinity!"

Spirit gazed upon their children with such love proclaiming this moment in time to be the beginning of a new relationship with life.

The New Journey

This group of souls began to prepare for this unknown adventure. The time came to leave, and the air was filled with tremendous excitement. These souls imagined traveling through the kingdom like a stallion about to race across an open prairie. The excitement and passion for this adventure filled the air with electrifying energy. Finally, these children of God said goodbye and exploded into a reality that lay just beyond the boundaries of the kingdom. The force of these souls, these Christed ones, created an enormous impact within their own consciousness. Love would not be contained within this boundless freedom. The magnificent souls divided into billions of aspects, honoring the intention that Spirit know itself as a multiple, unlimited reflection of itself. Each soul now perceived itself as individuated and yet interconnected. Interesting, is it not?

Waiting like a blank tapestry for these grand new creators was the void of creation. How would each of those aspects perceive themselves? This was a dramatic moment. Your identity shifted in a blink of an eye. Your sense of self and your new surroundings stimulated some new feelings. You had never experienced anything but love. You never felt disconnected from the Mother and Father of creation. And yet within this dark void, some aspects of your soul experienced a longing to return home. And as your efforts to return failed, your sadness turned to sorrow, anger, resentment, betrayal, and abandonment. For the first time you felt alone. You tasted fear.

Your only experience of any reality was your life within the kingdom. Some aspects held true to that reality and declared that to be your truth. The kingdom was your only reference. Many of you felt that you would honor this gift Spirit bestowed upon you by being true to the nature of a united consciousness, but other aspects of your soul simply could not shift their reaction to now feeling separate from the kingdom and Spirit. These aspects acknowledged these new feelings as being real but lacked any prior experience that would allow them to resolve these painful emotions. The billions of fragments began to resonate to the quality of energy that was being generated by the thoughts of each aspect. A preference for a perception was embraced which in turn served to divide your aspects into smaller groups. These groups became families, each with their own particular preference for an experience of reality that was supported by the thoughts and feelings of each aspect.

Light and Dark

Over time, those families that believed that the kingdom represented the only version of truth called themselves the light. In turn, this family of light turned to those aspects that were struggling with these new emotions and labeled their counterparts as being in the dark. They became the family of the dark. In so doing, duality was created and all of creation throughout all of the different galaxies was defined as such.

Now, this is not a story of right and wrong. It is an understanding of the nature of Spirit's gift. The nature of freedom, the nature of love itself. For Spirit could have added some criteria to this gift. Spirit could have insisted that if the soul ever divided, that like Spirit, it fall in love with its own reflection. However, this gift was offered without any conditions, no restrictions and, as well, no map to follow. There was but Spirit's own consciousness within every soul. That consciousness was deeply in love with its own reflection.

The relationship between the families of light and dark became very polarized. Conflict and confrontation became your preference of how each of you chose to relate to these different aspects of your self. This led to galactic wars beyond your imagination as a human being. Creating a dilemma for both families, life was not expanding in this dualistic experience. Love was being forced to be contained. Love, however, has its own nature. It was love and the fear that life will not survive this conflict that encouraged a grand meeting between these families. Survival motivated your attendance, and so a grand solution to your dilemma was proposed.

The Galactic Solution

You would seek to resolve the seeds of distrust by creating a planet that would act as a stage to find solution to your galactic dilemma. This planet has been called many names, but today it is known as Earth. You would create a reality where the reflection of each soul's thoughts and emotions would be unavoidable, giving each soul the opportunity to discover a solution to their internal conflict. The inhabitants of this planet would also have no memory of their past unless a solution was discovered. If the solution was discovered, the soul would openly share its experience that would serve the collective consciousness of both families.

Your past as a human being is your galactic story played out in your human affairs. All of your religions are based upon the translated life of those souls that did discover the very solution to your galactic conflict. They embraced and embodied the very consciousness within them that fell in love with its own reflection. They learned to love their brother/sister as themselves.

We can now speak to you in this way for you, soul, have discovered eons later a solution to your own journey. Love cannot be contained! You have embraced the light and dark within you. Your reality outside the kingdom now includes thoughts and feelings that never existed within the kingdom. You have validated these feelings and have discovered that love will support and heal it all. Loving your own reflection no matter the state of consciousness of that reflection has given you what you have been seeking. You feel within your blood the very presence of Spirit within your heart. The essence of the kingdom, Spirit, comes to you! Your willingness to explore the nature of a united consciousness within this dualistic environment invites a breath of fresh air into all of existence. It offers a new potential for all of creation to reunite. You, soul, playing the part of being human, are changing all of life, and you wonder why we are celebrating?

Your soul spent eons of time pursuing the energy to return back to your home. You developed technology, religions and cultures with the intent to leave this new landscape to experience once again the love that emanates from your Mother and Father; Spirit. You relied on your mind, your male nature, to try and figure out the best way to achieve and fulfill the yearning in your heart, and, as devoted as your mind is to your soul, you have discovered as a human being that the mind is not qualified for such a task. You have discovered, much to your minds relief, that the energy of Spirit, the kingdom, will come to you if you allow yourself to receive this presence. This is where we find many of you at this time. You are just beginning to shift your reliance on your mind by trusting your heart, your female nature, and you are learning to receive and feel the waves of love entering your body from the life that is all around you. You are learning to allow life to love its own reflection of itself -YOU.

In this allowance, you have become conscious of a wounded heart. You recognize the shields and filters that have served you for so long to protect a heart that feels disconnected from Spirit. Some of you have discovered that the presence of Spirit has no agenda. You are beginning to trust yourself in these vulnerable stages to feel love once

34

again. The shields you have created for your own protection will also exclude love. Each day of your life is now unraveling the reliance on your human mind, inviting a reunion, a divine marriage with the Heart and Mind of Creation. This presence in turn acts as a beacon resonating to the very qualities of joy, acting then as a magnet that allows for the embodiment of unity consciousness within your physical body.

Dear souls, it was you who volunteered for this grand adventure. Some of you are beginning to feel the excitement return, feeling the passion to co-create with the presence of Spirit within you. Some of you are allowing yourself to finally relax and allow the sweet, blissful presence of the kingdom to wash over you. And some of you, brave souls, are beginning to create with each thought and feeling a new experience of life. It is a life that joyfully celebrates the unlimited potentials to experience a love that cannot be contained.

You cannot imagine the celebration that is occurring on our side. We know your world is still immersed in turmoil and conflict, and we acknowledge that it is but a small minority of humans who have chosen to experience life outside the parameters of duality. And yet, this small group of devoted souls continues to create new potentials for all to see. They are offering to those with the heart and mind to listen a new perspective of life, a life whose foundation is built upon the love you have given to yourself. You have returned to something far greater than the kingdom. You have inherited the throne of your own creations when you recognize that you are Spirit also. You, soul, are the one who looked at its own reflection and fell deeply in love with itself. It is you, soul, who is being invited to own your birthright here as a human being. Christ consciousness - God consciousness. These words hardly describe your magnificence.

Ascension

Ascension is all about bringing the experience of Spirit into your physical reality, into your mundane day-to-day experiences, which then transcends your polarized relationship with life. Many of you use your spiritual path as a means for getting off this planet. It is our joy to remind you that the freedom you seek resides within the experience of the flesh. You will return to this environment until you have allowed the solution to become your physical experience. If physical reality was the pinnacle of creation, would you give yourself permission to truly enjoy it? This environment offers the potential to resolve what you were unable to resolve in the nonphysical dimensions.

Read these words again and again, and they will trigger a memory to resolve these feelings. Embrace it all! And in the openness of your heart, surrender your resistance. Your heart allows the presence of Spirit to come to you. You can literally feel Spirit dancing upon your body like raindrops, continuously raining upon your body. It is this state of consciousness that allowed Jesus to demonstrate for you, your heritage. From that perspective, all of you are the second coming of Christ consciousness if you too allow these raindrops to become your new diet. This diet will support whatever your heart desires by manifesting an abundance of joy that you deserve and are worthy of receiving now.

Many of you are waiting for a quantum leap into an ascended state of consciousness. You have declared this to happen during the year 2012. And yet, many of you said, "Why wait?" and have started to allow for this transformation to occur now. During this decade, there will also be millions - millions questioning reality/duality. They will turn to look and see who is living a life that has a new meaning, one that supports their questioning mind and awakened heart. Will you let these raindrops of Spirit support you and your service to your human family? Will you serve their process that allows them the freedom to discover a reality that is not polarized? Does such a service make your heart sing? It matters not what form that service takes. Can you openly share how it is that Spirit has come to you. Not from a place that would ask that you sacrifice your own self-fulfillment. This new type of service asks that these raindrops of energy continuously fill your life. Service is but the overflow that is shared. You will be challenged to love yourself in this way.

We honor you, soul. It is now time for you to honor you! Allow yourself to now receive the love that is all around you. Within these pages we will guide you back to your Self, all in the name of love. We hope you are prepared for the flood of hugs, tears of joy and laughter that will greet you when you leave this earth. History will always remember each of you for the work you are doing here. I, Michael, am forever in love with the beauty of that which has always resided within you. It is springtime in all of creation, blossom, soul, blossom for all to see!

Chapter Three

Befriending the Ego

At the core of your being is a vast identity or presence that supports your underlying perceptions. This is your divine nature, residing within your heart as a birthing place for all of your creations. This presence is experienced throughout all of creation as being the source of life. In our story of how Spirit fell in love with itself, this presence became known as the Heart and Mind of Creation. This divine nature is returning to you. It does not arrive with a predetermined agenda to make itself known to your reality-it has no agenda. Its arrival is solely based on your willingness to receive the clarity and grace of your own magnificence. The core of this book is about learning to receive this presence and to integrate that into your day-to-day reality.

Being in receivership is a way of life. It will challenge your notion of what is truly important, stirring up unresolved issues, while awakening dormant, intuitive abilities within your body. It will release chemicals within your glands that were designed to respond to Spirit. This presence will not only change how you perceive yourself, it will help resolve your inner conflicts. Spirit is here to love you. Many of you already feel it's presence while meditating, acting as a facilitator during your energy work, or when you allow joy to be your reality. Many others are but waiting for this presence to descend. Spirit, your divine male and female nature will not force itself upon any of you. Each of you will experience Spirit within your body through the relationship you have with your soul and human nature. This relationship will define with each breath, each moment, the very experience of your life. It is not a time for your soul to be complacent, passively allowing your past to dictate your future. It is a time for your soul to act as a wise mediator between all aspects of yourself. Together, let us explore this inner relationship, one that will allow you to truly taste the fruits of Spirit.

Who am I? It is a question that torments the mind of humanity. Gazing into a mirror, you want to believe that this is your soul looking back. A soul that has embodied all aspects of itself to represent its nature will reflect a dynamic presence that is undeniable. Some of you have seen this aspect of your soul and have discovered that your soul nature looks and feels very different from your conditioned human nature. For the most part, the identity you assume as being you is but a byproduct of your upbringing, your past experiences. It was created with a divine purpose to act as a witness to your soul's journey, to record and document, like a photographer, your experiences. You have within you a living library filled with accounts of your past for you to access at any time. This photographer is here to serve you, not control you. It has been called many names, including your personality or ego.

Discovering a solution to your galactic dilemma required some creative thinking. Reincarnating into a physical reality over and over gave your soul numerous opportunities to embrace its own resistance to loving its reflection. It gave you the time and space to set up potentials, prior to each incarnation, that would provide a stage

41

for your own self-discovery. A love for the multiple reflections of your self that would transcend a fear based reality. In your early childhood years, your soul would enter this world still feeling a strong connection with your angelic family. Over time, the pain of feeling undermined, misunderstood, ridiculed, and disrespected disturbed this connection. Your soul, unable to communicate clearly on its own behalf as a human child, discovered how to avoid these conflicts - you simply left your body. You experienced in your relationships with your parents, siblings, teachers and friends the most painful of encounters - love being withheld. For the most part, you felt this energetically, and like most adult humans, you learned the virtue of shielding yourself. Many of you survived very abusive physical and emotional upbringings. You adapted to your environment simply to survive. Your soul, during your childhood, would spend much of its time with us. For as a child, your relationship with your nonphysical family was still intact. Eventually we would became known as your imagination.

During those times when you literally left your body, another part of you assumed responsibility for your life. It was not qualified to take on this burden, but over time it would learn to represent you as best it could. This part is your 'grand photographer,' your ego/personality. It became your identity based on the documentation of all the pictures of your past experiences it took in your life, creating a grand photo album that it uses as a reference. It has befriended another part of you that also enjoys detailing and defining your life and it, as well, feels disconnected from the presence of Spirit. It is your human mind.

You, soul, spent much of your early years on earth keeping one foot in physical reality and one foot with us. When life on earth became too challenging, you would leave the difficult parts to your personality to handle. Having only your past to refer to, it learned to serve you by making the best choice it could to avoid situations that resembled past associations. This went on for some time, until the soul decided it was safe to be physically present and to stop avoiding the challenges you faced. As we perceive the sea of consciousness that is humanity, this relationship between your soul and personality is very polarized. It is a relationship that must be healed in order to experience the ecstatic presence of Spirit.

Your history would suggest that the healing takes the form of purging you of this photographer. As an adult, you perceive this one as being the root of the problem that must be eliminated. The ego, however, continues to serve you by protecting you from any experience that might trigger the pain of love being withheld. Every time you feel inspired to act on your heart's behalf, you also feel the resistance, distrust, and doubts of your ego wanting to protect you. Many of your therapies are attempting to address these fears without offering to establish a new, healthy relationship between the ego and the soul. The ego continues to shield your heart by projecting 'thought packages' into your interpersonal and global interactions. This leads us to ask: "If the denial of this relationship was your ticket to freedom dear soul, don't you think the train would have arrived by now?"

It is not our intention to belittle you. However, your grand photographer has solid evidence that this world is not a safe place to live in. It believes your ticket to feeling safe resides in your mind, shutting yourself off from your heart and not feeling the pain of this reality. This is very challenging for each of you, for you have discovered that the yearning in your heart can never be satisfied by the mind alone. No matter how many new and exciting concepts you intellectually discover, the heart continues to wait to experience self-fulfillment. Many of you are aware of these conflicting feelings within you. You also believe that they exist outside of you. If you could see this terrified little photographer trying its best to represent your soul nature, true compassion would swell in your heart.

Yes, it is serving you, and it has become angry and resentful. It gets blamed for everything you lack and never receives any recognition for the job that it does do very well. A dramatic shift is waiting in each of you that will ask the soul to get in the driver's seat of your life. Are you ready to assume full residence and responsibility for your physical experience, starting with the relationship many of you have yet to offer to your photographer? Are you, soul, ready to sign a lifetime lease agreement with your body?

While you were playing with us, your personality assumed responsibility for your own survival. It is not qualified nor did it agree to this relationship. But every time you jumped ship and came over to our side, someone had to keep the ship afloat. Now that you are back, you are embarrassed that this photographer has been representing you to the world. Are you ready to become a full-time resident here on planet earth? Being such creative thinkers, could you not use this very relationship between the ego and soul as an opportunity to discover the solution to our galactic dilemma and all of your past lives? Is it within your soul to love that which you judge to be unlovable? Would this not heal the very core of a polarized reality?

Don't take our word for it. Put it to the test. Start to embrace this little photographer as a reflection of your own fears and see if, with a little practice, you are not able to act on your heart's desires without all the resistance. This intimate relationship with this aspect of your soul nature will greatly accelerate your ascension experience.

Many of you are just beginning to recognize that you cannot experience this intellectually. It is a dream that becomes a new reality when the experience becomes tangible in every cell of your body. This new relationship will ask of you to place your attention on how you are feeling, and to acknowledge the concerns and doubts by not taking it personally. You, soul, can teach this photographer that this is indeed a safe world to live in which in turn empowers you. Your ego will only believe this to be true at face value. So, you have some teaching to do by giving it as many tangible experiences as you dare that are filled with a passion and joy for life. Your ego must 'photograph' these experiences and over time will begin to relax and trust that life is rewarding.

Now this can be quite enjoyable! Your task in life is to offer new and fulfilling experiences to your grand photographer each and every day to heal the reliance on the old photo album that is filled with painful or unfulfilling pictures. We, the Family of Michael, serve this new intention by igniting the inertia within you that has kept you complacent. We will say it again - this polarized relationship will not change unless you offer tangible evidence to your ego and mind that your heart can be trusted. It is not a time for your soul to be passive. Allowing Spirit into your life does not deny you the pleasures of living. Quite the contrary, it invites you to taste a passion for life that will transform your identity. Many of you yearn for this. It is very much our desire for you to know how this reunion can be realized in your day-to-day reality.

When you allow the energy of Spirit to come to you in this human experience, then you can have the multidimensional experiences of yourself here in physical reality. What is that going to do to all of you? How will that change your identity? How are you going to coexist in this collective dream with humanity, this dream that has you feeling diminished and separate from love?

How are you going to do this? We encourage you to do this by creating joy in your life. All of you are very familiar with the drama and trauma that is a byproduct of feeling disconnected from your joy. How would it feel if you truly trusted in your own heart and allowed your physical bodies to experience the joy and passion of life? Can you imagine the pleasure of feeling the support from the love that is within all of life? What happens when the presence of Spirit does come to us? It stirs and awakens within you your own divinity. How does your divinity represent itself as a human being? Not very well if you try to contain it within a polarized system. You already know how unfulfilling that experience can be. It is time to taste something new.

Some of you believe that you must perfect yourself before you are qualified to receive such a consciousness, that you must be enlightened before the energy of Spirit will enter your life. You know we very much enjoy playing with our partner (Robert). He is living proof that enlightenment is truly misunderstood. Many of you have spent years preparing yourself for this ascended state of consciousness, and much of that is to be honored. However, it is the service to your joy that will accelerate the integration of your divine nature into your day-to-day reality, allowing the ego to sit where it is comfortable - in the backseat.

We invite each of you to walk out of this old dream that is based in self-doubt and dis-trust. To walk into a new life, you must give it a birthing place within your heart, mind, and body. This new life will ask of you to be in the moment and to rely on the support you experience when you embody your divine nature. Learning to receive will invite you to redefine your identity. It will invite you to stay connected to the joy that supports you by being present. Being in this Now moment will challenge the mind, for your current identity is based almost solely on the patterns of thoughts that keep reinforcing your past history. It will challenge you, and yet with a little practice, the presence of Spirit will reveal itself.

You have within you the most powerful tool for expressing yourself in this moment. Your breath. Every breath is another opportunity to give your mind something to hang onto. Conscious breathing as a way of life is very powerful. What would your life be like if your devotion shifted to being in this moment? As you feel the air enter your nostrils, there is a presence as well that is waiting to enter every pore in your skin.

When you are present, not projecting your thoughts into the future or regurgitating your past, you open yourself to the sweet nectar of a pure love. You can learn to feel this presence simply by quieting the mind for 15—30 minutes, consciously breathing with each breath. With a little practice, you will begin to feel the presence of your angelic self. You can pray for it, hoping that it is real, but without putting this into practice, you keep that experience separated from your physical reality.

How will you relate to your friends, family and neighbors with your eyes blazing with the presence of an unconditional love? Do you fear society will perceive you as being deluded, out of touch with the real world? Will they think you are a drug addict when you are beaming with the presence of joy? Spirit comes to you when you learn to receive its presence. How will humanity understand this? They will not at first, so how will you respond?

Will you serve your human family, teach them with compassion? You can teach them that all of life is about making a choice. Choosing to be free, to feel, as you want to feel is a very empowering choice. How do we choose that? It starts here and now. What feeling would you choose at this moment? Can you imagine it and simply breathe that feeling into your body? What feelings are you willing to make the standard for your reality? What value do you place on yourself? It is your birthright to set the standard of your own reality. You can transform any state of consciousness within yourself. Can it be your joy to acknowledge your fears and transform them back into love? Each of you have this ability, and it is our joy to remind you of that. At this moment, there is a love that supports

ALL of life. It is available to you right Now. Can you allow it into your life and freely share it with those aspects that feel separate from love? There is a profound healing waiting for each of you. Your photographer will not trust this love at first. It can be your joy to witness the power of love as the fears of your ego begin to dissolve simply by offering love to them. This is not a sugar coated love. It is profound, unwavering, and direct.

This is a grand moment! It is just the beginning. It was only 18 years ago that we read the energy of this planet, and you in turn did something magnificent. You created a grand celebration called your Harmonic Convergence. Slowly the soul began to descend back into the body. You saw this as an opportunity to reunite globally even though you were ridiculed for being out of touch with reality.

You celebrated the opportunity even if it was just a hope that there is something more real than this dream of separation. You started to give life to a new dream from your heart. The integration of this new dream, a new vision, started to grow roots during the next three or four years. We could see then that you had created a new potential for humanity. There was not going to be the end times in terms of your species being terminated. You had discovered a key to your galactic dilemma and now it was time to bring it into reality. You changed the very fabric of your own future.

Once you got a taste of Spirit coming to you, you wanted to accelerate your ascension process. What once took a lifetime to digest, you attempted to do on a monthly or yearly basis. This is not by our doing. We are only supporting your intentions. It is your choice. You wanted to speed it up. In the speeding up there is a bit of exhaustion on the physical part that is questioning, "How do I integrate all these changes?" Your mind is saying, "It's not my problem. Deal with it."

And your heart is answering, "Indeed, why don't we relax and enjoy ourselves? How can I serve you both?" The body shares that when you are in joy, everything flows much easier. The ego shares that when its fears are validated, it does not seek to control your life. Your mind shares that when it feels the presence of its female counterpart in the body it does not feel responsible for the life of the soul.

When you finally relax into allowing Spirit to become a part of your life, you tap into your multidimensional nature. Living within that reality is your spiritual family. You move from the old dream where you believe you are a singular being having a singular headache from your human experience, into being a multidimensional representative of a galactic family. What is humanity going to do with this? You will have to teach them how it is that you transcended from this singular state of consciousness, an identity feeling separate from Spirit, to an identity that embodies God consciousness. This is your natural state of being when you embrace your divine nature - an identity that could not be contained. Within that love, every gland and cell of your body is coded to awaken. It begins to secrete the hormones that will bring your body back online, opening the seven seals, balancing the chakras, igniting the crystalline structures and dancing within the beauty of life itself.

What ignites the body biochemically? Joyful experiences! We know you resist this, all of you. And yet, this is your key. On a physical level, the cells are waiting for this new diet. A diet that will replace the cells that for too long have settled for what we call misery soup. That diet of misery soup is your past history, and from a physical standpoint, your body will go through its own resistance. The patterns of behavior that have developed from consuming endless bowls of misery soup support an entire community of cells. The solution? Conscious choices of activities and experiences that are supported by your own joy, repeated as often as you like. This supports a diet that is based on the pleasures of life.

These new joy cells will awaken your biology to the original blueprint of your physical body. Such a blueprint resonates with your divine nature. It will ignite a detoxing process (we know how much you love this stage) within the body to accommodate these newly awakened cells.

What fights such a good battle to protect you from knowing this truth? It is the nature of a polarized reality, with the personality being its witness. This beloved personality has photographed your human story and holds that as your truth. It knows your identity to be you're past history and it has a rather large photo album to make its case. Your past keeps repeating itself, lifetime after lifetime, if you don't trust in your own creative abilities.

Some of your spiritual teachings insist that this ego personality is the source of your resistance, and to achieve enlightenment, you must get rid of or overthrow that little puppy. You must annihilate it, for there is no freedom and no enlightenment unless you release this one. How are we doing with that?

This ego personality, for most of you, will be the most humbling experience any of you will ever have. It brings the greatest shame to you, and that is an old dream. That is a very old dream. You now have the tools and freedom to experience life in any manner you desire. Can you discern for yourself who you are representing in this moment? Are you the soul of a grander self or is it that little puppy again? Your personality is very loyal to you. When you get clear about owning your God self and making that relationship tangible, it will serve your new allegiance. How do you discern if indeed it is your personality?

This photographer has an agenda to protect you. It is very quick to defend that agenda. It serves you by protecting you from a world that is not safe. It has all your past experiences recorded in a photo album as living proof that to survive, the shields must be up at all times. And based on your past history, your personality is right.

Until you give it a new experience that demonstrates that life will support your heart's desires, it will continue to act as your protector. It needs to see tangible proof, and so we are encouraging you to give it physical evidence that joy is real. Allow yourself to receive the energetic nutrients from life all around you. This is a love without boundaries, borders or shields. As you practice feeling how life truly loves you, turn to this photographer and share what you are learning to receive for yourself.

Your personality seeks to be recognized for the job it is doing. Its security is very fragile until you have developed within yourself a conscious loving relationship with life. Until you turn within and have this new relationship, it will project its insecurities into other people to get a response simply for the recognition. Many of you have found yourselves embarrassed by the level of control this one has in your life. As children, you sincerely appreciated its role as your protector. As an adult, would this not be a good time to change that relationship? Indeed!

This personality would say to all of you: "I know that while I was in the driver's seat, we found ourselves in the ditch wallowing in self-pity, but you are still alive, are you not? Where is the gratitude for my willingness to at least attempt to steer your life while you were away playing with the angels?"

It is also the one now saying; "I do not want to be responsible any longer for assuming the role of your magnificence, for I cannot do that for you. I feel utterly unqualified, and it is embarrassing to us both when you put me in that position. We must have a new relationship, a relationship that is based on you allowing yourself to feel the magnificence of who you are and sharing that with me, your photographer. In this new relationship, I would ask of you to heal the past by acknowledging the emotional scars that exist in our heart. Then I can relax and do what I do very well in the back seat of your life—take pictures."

"I am devoted to you, soul, and until you initiate joyful experiences that support your magnificence, then I, your personality, have nothing tangible to validate that this joy business is real, that it is not just a bunch of fairy tales. You must give me tangible experiences to photograph that are supported by joy for me to lower the shields."

It is time to give this personality a new photo album that is based on multiple opportunities that you create for yourself that allows life to share its love with you. Love yourself so deeply that you are willing to receive that love. Imagine a new photo album that is solely based on self-love. That sounds like a new dream, a new paradigm, a new consciousness, and a real solution to a polarized history. Your job is to discover such a love for your own reflection that you recognize that reflection as being God/Goddess looking back at you as itself. Can you sense why we are so involved with celebrating what you are doing with your life at this time in history? Multiple reflections of God's love for itself? You have no idea of the gratitude all of creation has for each of you!

What lies ahead for you as you become the presence of Spirit incarnate? What is your most responsible agenda as a human being? To enjoy life? Does this feel responsible? Put your imagination to work. Give your personality tangible evidence that this is real and sincere. Every single day, schedule the most delightful, joyful, ecstatic experience you can imagine having for yourself. Then, do it, even to the objection of those in your life who are still enjoying the misery soup. Do it to the objection within you that is saying, "This is not real, how can I enjoy my life when the world is in such pain?" By giving yourself permission to make it that real.

This is the new dream, making it so real you can taste it! Can you wake up from your diminished dream of life and recognize that love is alive in everything? What would you become if you would devote one hour a day to joyfully existing? Just one hour a day. We would say you would become a human angel. Not quite ready to be God/Goddess yet? One hour a day doesn't quite cut it, but the human angel will most definitely separate you from the misery soup diet. It is time. It is time to make it real.

At this time on earth, there is but two percent of humanity that is saying, "I will do anything, anything to reclaim my angelic heritage. Everything else is just an old dream. Everything else is feeling as if it is an illusion, and this time I do not want to spend my entire life in a cave meditating on this. I do not want to isolate myself in a monastery. I do not want to separate myself from the rest of my family playing the shaman."

You are seeing how many of your friends, family members, and co-workers are really struggling with maintaining a false sense of self-love. Are you willing to be of service to this new love? We believe you are. You do not need to twist the arms of ignorance to make your new vision tangible. Those who are ready for Spirit will come to you. The misery soup diet that is based on guilt and shame will become indigestible to many.

What is your homework? What is this new spiritual teaching that is so demanding of you? Enjoy your life each moment, every hour, and if you are not, then you are choosing to remain unconscious of your birthright. Your new allegiance to a life that honors joy, self-love and self-fulfillment will look very, very vain to those eyes that understand love from a place of sacrifice and denial.

You were the ones who had the courage to face the feelings that much of creation has disowned, to create a solution to our galactic story, our old dream. In the hundreds and thousands of lifetimes you have experienced as a human being, your journey has culminated in this one life. It is all very new. Now what do we do with it? We cultivate it. We cultivate it every day by being conscious of how we are feeling.

Self-love supports this new foundation with life and asks of you to take responsibility for maintaining this connection with love. That connection begins with opening your life and your body to feeling the energy of life supporting you, filling every cell in your body with this love. As you learn to receive this love for yourself, what you will share is the overflow radiating from your eyes, your entire body.

Your magnificence will shatter the mirrors that you look into each morning, breaking the illusions of who you are with the radiance of love that is connected to all of life. It is for each of you to discover this. We will share our presence with all of you in any way that you will allow this relationship to blossom. When you allow it to blossom, you will understand that we are not the exalted ones. We did not raise our hands when it was time to volunteer to come to earth. To volunteer to adapt to the very parameters of a fear-based reality so as to demonstrate to your human and galactic family the very solution to any polarized reality.

How much joy are you willing to have in your life? How many tangible experiences will you give this personality so that it will learn to trust that it does not need to be filtering energy? It does not need to protect you from having fulfilling, passionate relationships. It does not need to endure occupations that are boring. It does not serve you by putting up endless shields that protect you from a belief that life is not safe.

It is a wondrous time to be on earth. If you are willing to place a value on your life that honors self-love, you will experience in your physical reality what your heart has yearned to taste for eons of time. Befriending your ego plays an important role that serves the integration of your divinity. Are you ready to receive the love that exists in life all around you at this moment? If that is a yes, we suggest you buckle your seatbelts for the love wash of your life!

Chapter Four

A New Foundation

Your experience on earth has always been about re-
solving a polarized relationship with life. This lifetime
offers a most profound opportunity to reunite with the divided aspects of your own consciousness. This unification
of your Self reawakens within each of you a natural state of
being—self-love. It is our joy to serve this love by reminding you of how you may receive this gift in your day-to-day
reality. The gift of love is your birthright! There is nothing
you need to prove or demonstrate to receive love. It offers
itself to you just as you are at this moment.

When you choose love for yourself, you strengthen the foundation for a new life on earth—a foundation that honors all of life. We stand before each of you, deeply respecting your devotion to allow your life to be rewarding and fulfilling.

We serve you by igniting the passion within your heart to burn the inertia that denies you the very elixir for your polarized reality. Self- awareness acknowledges your mind, body, ego, soul, and the Heart and Mind of Creation. You become devoted to self-fulfilling experiences. By igniting your passions, you become conscious of the power of choice. It begins with you, dear soul. Will you allow the perfection of your human nature to be loved?

The wounded heart of a human being has become epidemic. Each of you has experienced the pain of love being withheld. For most of humanity, that wound never truly heals during their lifetime. You survived feeling disconnected from love in part by developing shields or energetic band-aids that are used to protect the exposed and vulnerable condition of a heart that feels violated. These violations or uninvited intrusions into your heart created the belief that love equals pain. The pain of love being withheld is so severe, most of you choose to shut down your emotional body. You discovered safety in your mind by developing an intellectual perspective that confined your love to well-intended concepts and ideals. These shields created an energetic cocoon around your body, keeping the unspoken agendas of others from tampering with your feelings.

Many of you have and are just beginning to respond to a spiritual awakening that invites you to open your heart and feel the presence of Spirit. At face value, this invitation seems harmless and yet not all spiritual paths are supported by the presence of Spirit. Your heart yearns to reconnect with life, to once again feel the continuous flow of love that naturally shares itself with all of life. Interfering with that desire are the very shields you put in place to protect this vulnerable heart.

We deeply respect your dilemma. To trust that it is safe to receive love will require that the shields come down. They have served you well but they also filter or diminish your connection to energies that honor and respect a sovereign heart.

It is an awkward place you find yourself in. Many spiritual teachings invite you to open your heart without addressing the energetic exchange that violated the heart. Can you allow yourself to be so vulnerable to trust that your heart will not be violated again? We have shared that your grand photographer is already working overtime with its agenda to protect you. How do you allow the expansion of your heart? You are learning to create for yourself an energetic foundation that supports your new emerging self. This new foundation will be continuously reinforced by your devotion to self-love. A love for self that will dramatically change how you interrelate and interact with each other.

The patterns of behavior that reinforced the concept of shielding were a byproduct of a horizontal energetic exchange or connection between you and life. You are learning to discern the difference between extracting energies and the art of blending or merging energies. This book represents the merging of an angelic family with a human being. How you choose to share your love now comes from a place where you have actively chosen to fulfill your own desires. Self-fulfillment does not require anyone else to make your life more fulfilling. It acknowledges your sovereign right to experience life in any way you would choose for yourself.

Horizontal Connection

It is this horizontal connection that has you feeling dependent on what others expect of you, both personally and collectively. These expectations ask that you compromise your own desires and develop an understanding of love that is based on self-sacrifice. And how is that diet going? In your horizontal connection with life, you have learned to take energies to fulfill your own desires. The most sacred of all your energetic expressions resides within your sexuality. Here, you have reduced this most potent expression of creativity to mere physical stimulation. You have at your disposal the very gift of creation. Adapting to this horizontal relationship, you deny yourself the experience of merging and blending with Spirit in communion with another. This is your heritage and perhaps the most potent way for a human to experience the presence of Spirit. Such is the awkwardness of two lovers that have yet to discover a vertical connection by looking at one another to fulfill their inner desires. Your horizontal connections reinforce a feeling that you don't deserve love. They support a long held belief that love must be earned before you receive it.

At the core of your heart is a deep yearning to return home, to the kingdom. You have spent eons of time trying to figure out how to get back to the blissful and serene environment of the kingdom. Having experienced such a dramatic and painful disconnection from your home, you engaged in numerous experiments hoping to reestablish that connection in your personal relationships. Let us step back for a moment and simply observe the relationship you have with your planet.

Extracting Energy

How are your basic needs provided for each of you? You desire the comfort of a home which requires resources/materials to build the structure. We are not judging you for your need for shelter, for it serves you very well, but we do want to highlight the very nature of your horizontal relationship to create these shelters. Look at your home, the frame that supports it, the wall coverings, flooring material, roof, and windows. How were these materials obtained? Was there recognition that all of life is sacred or were these materials simply extracted from their source? Many of you have discovered that by borrowing from the wisdom of your native traditions, you can integrate these attitudes into your modern decision-making.

Let us look at your diet, which again, is not to say that it is wrong to enjoy food. Indeed it is a great pleasure. And yet how were your foods obtained? How do you prepare them? How are you feeling when you ingest them? Is there a deep reverence for the life that freely shares itself with you? Is there a mutual respect or have you become uncon-scious of that relationship and simply consume what you need? Isn't 'consumer' an interesting term? How would you approach your food and welcome it into your body from an understanding that your food is also Spirit?

Again, this is not about guilt or shame; nor is it about being in denial. It is about becoming conscious of how you literally feed yourself energetically, emotionally, and physically. How would humanity create living structures if raw materials were not extracted from the earth to provide that comfort? How would you design your vehicles if re-sources were not extracted from its source? How would you change your relationship to those things that support you if you offered mutual respect for the life that is sharing itself with you? Does joy have a place in all of this? We believe it does, for the earth provides you with a very tan-gible environment to resolve your interactions with all of life. You can have all that you desire, and it can be mani-fested into your life without extracting it from life. Some of you would say that we are suggesting you return to living in caves. We are not. We are suggesting that you already live in a cave of your own making and invite you to change your perception so you can enjoy the fruits of a life based on mutual respect. Your relationship to the natural resources of this planet is but a reflection of your relationship with your inner resources.

Vertical Relationship

This new awareness invites you to shift your horizontal connection with life to a vertical relationship. In this manner of relating, you allow life to come to you by feeling its presence downloading into your body. From this perspective, your body becomes a reservoir for the energies of life that support you. Jesus, as a human being, often spoke for the presence of 'The Christ.' In this state of consciousness, he was most powerfully vertically connected with 'Thy Father's Mansion'—the kingdom. The presence of Spirit would literally descend, merge, and blend with his thoughts, emotions, and body. In this relationship with Spirit, Jesus stated that: "All that I am, you are as well." Our service to each of you is to remind you of this powerful truth. Having a direct relationship with Spirit invites you to leave the polarized, horizontal connections and reconnect with the energy that supports all of life. This is your heritage. It has nothing to do with deserving. Reconnecting with the energies that support life is a powerful, sovereign relationship. It is not based on need. Life will naturally complement what you are willing to give to yourself. Horizontal connections are dependent on pursuing, trying, or forcing love to be in your life. A vertical relationship invites, allows, and is open to receiving love.

As you learn to feel these energies pouring into the top of your head, they, in turn, settle into every cell of your body. This vertical connection also extends into the center of the earth, allowing for the energies of Gaia to support you through your feet, the base of your spine, and your entire body. A vertical connection is the energetic template for a self-fulfilled individual. Your needs are not extracted or manipulated from other people or from the earth. Your relationship with the natural resources of this planet reflects your relationship with your own inner resources. In this new connection, you will learn to take responsibility for your own feelings and discern how it feels when you are connected to Spirit. With a little practice, you will discover that this connection is not restricted to a vertical entry but can circle in and around your entire body. We are suggesting that you begin this new manner of relating in a vertical fashion by consciously disconnecting from the entangled horizontal patterns.

Earth, then, is acting as a stage for all of you to experience the physical byproduct of your emotional desires. If you are 'feeling' disconnected from Spirit—you are! It is only recently that these horizontal cords have been detected by your science. Many courageous individuals left prominent occupations to deepen their awareness of these energetic patterns. Plugging into each other to fulfill your personal needs is a violation of your sovereign nature.

This new foundation will feel like a breath of fresh air, bringing with it a sense of freedom and excitement. Your heart will open and you will begin to experience how life wants to support you. When you create a spiritual foundation that is vertically connected, nature begins to play with you. You will begin to feel the wind caressing your cheeks to remind you that Spirit loves you. You will learn to bask in the warmth of the sun, fully understanding that you are receiving a reflection of your own self-worth. You will dance in the rain, celebrating a love for life because you have allowed life to love you back. These elements and all of nature can serve your longing to feel connected with Spirit. We highly recommend that you befriend nature in this way. It will be several generations before humanity has developed the emotional maturity to offer themselves in a spiritual communion. Nature, however, is ripe and waiting for a new communion with humanity.

In other lifetimes, the energy around your planet was so dense that it would literally sever this vertical connection. It made it very difficult for us, your nonphysical family, to merge with and support your experiences. Such is the power of a collective shield that is supported by fear. Our support became faith-based as you began to rely on prayers, hoping that someone up there was listening. Your prayers have been answered! You have lowered your shields just enough to allow love to enter your reality. The more you practice 'receiving' this presence, the more you can trust in the nature of love. Spirit has no agenda. It does not seek to rid you of your darkness. It offers itself to those fears so they may know the true character of love.

Now perhaps you feel more of our excitement, for the veil that has separated us for eons of time has thinned allowing once again for a bridge to exist between your physical world and our etheric world. How do you maintain this bridge? You choose to stay out of duality by maintaining this vertical connection and feed yourself with joyful experiences that YOU give to yourself. The loving feelings that come to you are but a reflection of your own love for yourself. Self-fulfillment will look vain to those who have yet to question duality. That is not your problem. Your sovereign nature is your heritage and birthright. Stop negotiating its worth by allowing yourself to become entangled in a web of confusion.

A polarized reality will invite you to play the victim, reinforcing your shields with distrust and doubt for the simple price of your own freedom. Is that still digestible dear soul? Are you ready to awaken from the pain and struggle so as to taste a passion for living? Many of you have discovered and are beginning to live this new awareness. Your soul is beginning to feel the very presence of the kingdom here on earth, but not because you have forced it into your life. You have learned to receive the very essence that supported life in the Kingdom. You have discovered that Spirit comes to you! Each day you awaken to the realization that, with this new foundation, being in receivership allows you now to have whatever your heart desires. That, soul, was the gift Spirit offered to all of you. It was not intended to become a burden. Are you feeling worthy of such a gift? Earth is the perfect place to resolve that conflict. Do you believe you deserve such a freedom? Earth, this most beautiful reality, gives you a splendid opportunity to realize that for yourself. If you had the freedom to go anywhere in all of existence to resolve your inner conflicts, where would you go? You have that freedom and you chose wisely!

Your Body in Turmoil

Now your challenge is to enjoy the fruits of your labors. The pain and discomfort in your body will heal as you shift from one perspective to another. Your body has the ability to accommodate this new foundation. We know it is testing your patience, but it has its own wisdom. Within your body is a community of cells; many are supported by your addiction to maintaining polarized horizontal connections with life. New cells are being introduced every second to accommodate your devotion to whatever beliefs you want to entertain. Loving yourself consciously will greatly accelerate your desire to experience more joy in your life. Your body will serve you, giving you feedback as your devotion to self-love expands or contracts. Your immune system is shifting from defending itself to allowing life to support you. Befriend these beautiful bodies. They are very loyal to your own fulfillment. The mind, only knowing a polarized reality until you introduce tangible evidence that another one exists, will interfere with this process initially. Self-love is also loving the mind, and for many of you, the love shared with the mind can best be described as 'tough love.'

There are many at this time who are contemplating a new life that is supported by a new foundation, a foundation that will encourage new beliefs. This does not come to you simply because you intend or affirm its presence. Being passive or complacent is still swimming in a polarized reality. Being conscious of how you are feeling is a very focused and grounded state of mind. It took many years for you to adapt to a diminished state of consciousness that supports itself by extracting from life. Do you have within you the compassion to allow for this new foundation to gradually begin to support you? It is a foundation built on your day-to-day choices. A quantum leap will not instantly manifest such a change for you. But as you shift your allegiance to self-love, in time it will feel you have leapt from one identity to another. How many ways would you like to know yourself as a human being? This new foundation will support all of your choices as long as they are based on self-love. As you say on Earth; "Tough job but someone has to do it."

As you learn to integrate these new choices, then I, Archangel Michael, can begin to grow new wings. The game of extracting, opposing and confronting, required that you needed such an angel to protect you. How might I serve you, dear soul, without my grand sword? What shall become of our relationship when you no longer need protection? I will joyfully follow your imagination into the very core of your heart, and there I will dance with you as your new friend. How do you like to dance, soul?

Chapter Five

A Sacred Relationship

The story of your soul, your divine journey since you left the kingdom, is filled with adventure, excitement, and conflict. Your grander self helped to create the stars, galaxies, and multiverses. The formless luminous presence of Spirit has always been with you. It has never left you. We share this with you to stir the memories of your own magnificence and to reawaken your relationship to a grand angelic lineage that is available to all of you—a relationship that will honor and respect the creative abilities of a human and an angel that have joined hands as sovereign beings.

Many of you have read stories of your past that share a galactic history that is grand. As much as you would like to believe that your origins come from the stars and that your abilities are truly unlimited, you continue to struggle with the day-to-day demands of being a human being. Confined to a physical body, many of you now yearn to return to the stars to play in the angelic realms that you imagine would fulfill your desire to be free. And yet, physical reality gives you the opportunity to discover the limitations and conditions you inherited and have carried with you since you left the kingdom. You are here, dear soul, to experience the integration of your divine aspects. To then turn and face humanity with your many gifts, with eyes that are blazing, with a sovereign heart, supported by a love for self.

In other lifetimes you would choose to incarnate into families that would encourage a relationship with Spirit and earth. Some of these cultures you have labeled as being native. You recognized prior to this lifetime that humanity would dismiss your awakened presence if you walk among them as a shaman from another culture. Being the clever and courageous souls you are, you understood that the mass consciousness of humanity would encourage you to separate your human nature from Spirit. You would be encouraged to compromise your freedom while playing the victim.

In time, you would awaken from this separation and begin to reunite your human mind with the Heart and Mind of Creation/Spirit. Many of you are experiencing this intense transformation as you read these words. By allowing your human mind to now serve your heart, you can consciously share with humanity a model of a fulfilled human being in whatever manner that brings you joy.

New Dreamer

We are speaking to the new dreamers, the ones who are willing to embody your divine nature. Each of you understands you now have the freedom to feel or experience life in any manner you desire. We celebrate your choice to activate this awareness by fully engaging in becoming very, very sensitive to how your body is feeling. These beautiful vessels are not a prison for your soul. They are devoted, divine companions offering the inner resources to experience whatever state of consciousness you would like to embody. If you want to embody the state of consciousness that created the stars, then you must embrace your divine nature. You must embrace a passion for living that now recognizes that your past no longer dictates your choices for you. Your past now serves you by merging with your expanded identity. This new identity is supported by your joy for living a life you always dreamed could be real.

Singing the Blues

We understand that the current collective conscious-ness of humanity has many of you 'singing the blues.' You believe that the majority rules, and until the majority chooses joy, then you must continue playing the victim. We invite you, simply for the fun of it, to put that belief to the test. Align your body with a state of consciousness that is deeply in love with itself. This is very much in the minority on your planet. Would you not agree?

To embody such a consciousness, one would make deliberate choices that are fulfilling and rewarding. In time, one will begin to experience the personal fulfillment of such a relationship. We invite you, as you embody this new relationship, to now place yourself in an environment where others have yet to taste this new joy for life. As you have shared with us on many occasions, that will not be hard to find.

If the majority rules, then how do you explain the relationship that spiritual teachers have with the majority of humanity? If you agree that they embody a state of consciousness that is very much in the minority, why doesn't the majority rule in their life? What choices have they made that allows them to interact with your reality and yet seemingly not be a part of it? We would suggest that for many of them, they made a choice, a preference for a reality that served their own relationship with Spirit.

Our companion is faced with the same choice as all of you - engage with life, people, and things from a polarized perspective or embody a new perspective that supports what many would label as his imagination. In his relationship with us, his soul family, the majority of humanity does not recognize this relationship, and yet, he is fulfilled.

Self-love is a true sovereign state of being. Self-love would ask each of you: "Why is it any of your business what other people are doing with their lives?" We invite you to experiment with these ways of selfishly loving yourself first and to see how your perspective of physical reality takes a quantum leap.

Down the Aisle at the Sunset

Many of you sense that the sun is setting on a life that is polarized. Opposing life is only perpetuating the very conflict that is so distasteful to many of you. We understand your deep and earnest desire for peace and cooperation between individuals, families, and nations.

Indeed, if the sun is truly setting on your collective reality, then each of you has discovered that the source for such a peace lies within your own heart. You are acknowledging that within you there are two, potent divine lovers. You are creating a magnificent marriage that reunites these lovers and allows for a sovereign and whole experience.

Walking down the aisle alongside this setting sun is your own male and female nature. It is a most sacred ceremony, ending the internal conflict between your mind and heart. As you embrace these aspects of yourself, you awaken the divine seed that has always been within you. For within each of you resides the very gift of creation. It is a gift that was freely shared by the Divine Mother and Father Spirit or God/Goddess. There is a presence that supports the majority of life if you will but allow it into your life.

The Heart of Creation / Sacred Feminine

In the kingdom, there existed a presence that literally blessed all of your experiences. You knew this presence by the underlying state of bliss that weaves its way into all of your thoughts and actions. This was the Divine Mother, the Sacred Feminine, or as we call her, the Heart of Creation. You have searched far and wide to reconnect with this presence. She is here now, within the pages of this book, offering her love to the one who is reading these words. She impregnates nature with her vitality, warmth, and passion. You can feel her in your home, at work, and igniting all of your personal relationships with a simple truth - the love you seek and yearn to feel is within you. The heart of this book is to teach and remind you that she makes herself known by your willingness to receive her presence. She embraces a universal truth - "All of Life is Sacred."

Her presence touches your heart and asks of you, "May I be with you, Beloved? I am that presence that exists before time and space. I join you now with my beloved male companion, your divine mind. I exist that love may be served. How may I serve you, dear soul? Are you ready to receive what has always been offered? My patience is eternal, but your pain need not be. Turn your attention inward, and like a gentle breeze, let me caress and soothe your tender heart. All is well. It is but your resistance that perpetuates the illusion of being separate from your divine heritage. I am not here to change the world. I am here to love life for I am life. As each of you accommodate this love for yourself, indeed, all of reality will change."

"I am ready to enter your life with each breath. Lay down your swords, your judgments, and your fears and receive the gift that was freely offered. My Beloved partner, the Mind of Creation or Father Spirit is also rejoicing as the soul of the human is allowing us to dance 'our dance.' Thank you, your path is now paved in joy. Blessings!"

The Search Ends

It is here on earth that you, soul, have discovered a new relationship within yourself. You are beginning to take responsibility for developing a conscious relationship with your divine male and female aspects. You are discovering that your human mind feels overwhelmed with the responsibility to fulfill your needs and desires. It is so devoted to you, soul, that it will attempt to steer your life using all of its human attributes. Residing within you is also a divine mind and heart. Your divine mind does not judge, ridicule or undermine your character. It embraces serving the Heart

84

of Creation by offering a detailed, close up view of life from a finite perspective.

If you are asking your human mind to read this book, it will search in vain for more details and stories to validate our words. It will use your own past as its only reference for deciding what is true. It waits for you, soul, to allow the presence of your divine nature to merge with its identity. When you hesitate or resist Spirit, the human mind goes back to serving you with its distorted perception.

Your human mind and personality are truly devoted, but without the presence of its divine counterparts, it becomes confused and disoriented. For, unlike your heart, it does not perceive the bigger picture. Your dilemma is to stop relying on the human mind to give you what only your divine nature can embody - unlimited, intuitive, and all encompassing perspectives. No divisions, no right or wrong, black or white, good or evil. It is ALL INCLUSIVE in its perception of reality. The majority of humanity is allowing itself to be ruled by the controlling influence of your conditioned past. Again, the human mind is very loyal and continues to serve you, knowing it has no clue when you ask what the purpose of life is?

Pick up The Phone

The mind is sensing that many of you are beginning to acknowledge its concerns. If you prefer to call this your awakening, indeed that is a beautiful description. In a way, you are simply picking up a phone that has been ringing for a very long time. You say, "Hello," and hear a barrage of complaints from your human mind asking and pleading, "Where is our divine nature? You keep asking me to make your life safe, known, and secure when I do not have a clue." The nature that your mind is referring to is the Heart and Mind of Creation.

Your female nature is endowed with a presence that brings a profound clarity to your thoughts—a perception that does not rely on thinking. This can be very confusing to your human experience and so we invite you again to put it to the test. Stop your internal dialog for 10-15 minutes and notice what part of you is now perceiving your life. Where did all the anxiety go? Why do you suddenly feel so content?

As a human being you will feel the presence of your female nature when you rely on your intuitive abilities to acknowledge her, trusting your feelings to guide you through your life. We know that the state of consciousness that you adapted to has undermined your feelings. You learned to rely almost exclusively on logic and reason. And yet, even logic would confirm that your collective reality lacks solutions to the many problems you face. Logic cannot confirm that Spirit is real. You only ridicule the very nature of your human mind with such questions. It can, however, give you a very detailed description of pieces or a slice of Spirit. Of course, there can be enormous pleasure in dissecting these slices, but it becomes dysfunctional when you are relying on the describer to take responsibility for the indescribable. Give that responsibility to your divine nature in partnership with your human mind, body, and soul, and watch your personal reality blossom.

Many of you are discovering that when you rely on your female nature or heart to answer your questions about life, it leaves you speechless. You develop a sense of knowing that is very difficult to describe even for the describer. And yet your divine mind, being most comfortable when it is truly connected to her presence, will joyfully attempt to describe her magnificence. Your divine male nature is at peace with itself by serving its counterpart, the divine female nature! This is not a gender-based relationship. You are using your human nature and physical reality as a place to experience and express this divine reunion within yourself.

Being in Receivership

We do not ask of any of you to take this at face value. We encourage you to experience it for yourself. Feel the dynamic presence of these divine lovers merging with each other in your physical reality. Why don't we start with your body as an anchor point for this reunion to unfold. What does that ask of you in order to allow such a grand reunion? It asks of you to learn to be in receivership. For your divine counterparts will not force their presence upon any of you. They have no agenda. You can pray with all your might till your face turns blue, but if you have not learned the fine art of receiving, you will feel that your prayers have not been answered. Not because they have not been heard, but because you are asking your human mind to create joy in your life. And how is that going?

Your mind has been pursuing, achieving, pushing, and controlling your life, in service, to help you feel fulfilled. You deny yourself the very experience you desire each and every time you ask your mind to create that experience for you. It wants to get in the backseat, but its devotion to you, soul, will not allow it to get back there until it feels your divine presence, Spirit in your body.

For most of you, this will be very challenging for some time. We know how unfulfilled life feels for many of you, and yet, shifting your allegiance to your divine nature can feel very vulnerable at first. Let us play with this new relationship and reveal some exciting possibilities that any of you can learn to enjoy.

The Joy of Receiving

We have asked our companion (Robert) to share in our workshops the practice of being in receivership. It simply invites you to spend 30 minutes each day, 3 times a day being still and imagining that life is loving you. If, at first, three times day is difficult to arrange, start with once a day. Imagine that at this very moment, all of nature is receiving love from the sun, moon, stars, and galaxies. It freely shares its fulfilled radiance from this relationship with all of you. There are no conditions and nothing to prove. You are qualified just as you are right now. Imagine, as you once did as a child, playing with this new idea that love enjoys taking the form of nature—the sun, wind, and rain. Love will not be contained and enjoys sharing itself with anyone who is open to being loved. Now to feel this presence, you as well must love yourself.

Morning Practice

Let us take this a step further. What are the first thoughts you hear when you start your day? Do they have anything to do with joyfully anticipating your day to come? If not, perhaps all these concerns are simply your mind feeling overly responsible for your life. Can we give it the break it is asking for? Play with some new thoughts just for the fun of it, and see how it changes your day.

Now the true delights of your day begin. Every form you call physical reality is but a description of one aspect of the Heart of Creation. It is a description of one aspect of her body for you to reflect upon. How many ways can you perceive her presence in your reality? Most of you start your day washing your body. As you jumped out of bed, your feet touched the floor. How did that feel? Did you notice how sensuous the floor feels to your feet? As you brushed your teeth, did you notice that your gums truly relish being brushed? How did that escape your attention? Are we still asking the mind to try and figure it out? You turned on a faucet to bring you water; did you stop and let yourself truly feel the texture of your metals that you call a faucet or were you thinking about where you will be later in the day, missing out on another opportunity to feel the presence of Spirit in your life?

Standing under the water, play with imagining how water is but another form love takes to share its presence with you.

Are you laughing and singing while she cleans your body and refreshens your Spirit? How long are you willing to let love, in the form of water, love you? What value are you willing to place on self-love? You end your shower by drying yourself with a towel. You guessed it; did you truly enjoy feeling the towel touch every part of your most sacred temple? Or, were you thinking that it is more important to treat it like a task, being very efficient to prepare yourself for being more productive. How is being productive going?

Some of you return to your bedroom to dress yourself. Here you get to choose colors and textures that will enhance and highlight your day. Dressing yourself is another wonderful opportunity to feel life loving you. How do the colors of your clothes make you feel? Can you sense how your body is more comfortable with certain fabrics? Do you enjoy experimenting with those choices?

Let us fast forward to your breakfast. Here again the pleasures of life confront you with a choice. Will you mindfully devour your food perhaps reading while you eat? Or is there in your food the opportunity to feel the presence of life loving you? For there is nothing you can eat on this planet that did not come from the Earth. This planet is yet another form of love that freely offers itself so that you might embrace your own reflection! How would you, yourself, like to be devoured? Respectfully, consciously, and with great appreciation?

What Is Your Preference?

The start of your day offers countless opportunities to reunite with Spirit by opening yourself to feel the love that is already here to serve you. Many of you have shared that if you embodied this type of awareness, you would not be able to continue with your present life. Do you have a preference? Do you enjoy 'feeling' alive? Life will always say "yes" by honoring your preference. It faithfully responds to your feelings of lack or abundance. It does not judge. It simply responds to your freedom to choose how you want to experience life. A life that is truly fulfilling will ask of you to be attentive and to not fall asleep at the wheel, letting your mind drive your life for you. This is a very sacred relationship that will demand all of your attention.

You have chosen to face the most difficult challenge as a human being—to fall in love with yourself by allowing your divine nature to support you. Being complacent and passive will not reunite these divine aspects within you. It will challenge you to love yourself as you have never loved before, for being in receivership is all about self-love.

When you learn to receive love, you will discover that these elements are all interconnected to your soul. This brings us back to Spirit dividing and perceiving its own reflection and falling in love with its Self. That experience continues through each of you. How many ways are you willing to love your own reflection at the start of each day? If joy became your new preference that all of life must serve, what value have you placed on joy in your personal relationships, occupations, and physical vitality? Loving yourself becomes the new authentic model for an emerging culture that has discovered a solution to a polarized existence.

All of this naturally leads us to ask the big question: Do you really want to take victimhood for a ride around the block one more time? Or, are you willing to receive the unlimited expressions that love has to offer in everything that is in your life right now? A self-empowered sovereign soul takes full responsibility for their experience of life. This lifetime offers a wonderful opportunity to stop hoping and start knowing you are Spirit also.

Life can become your love affair with your Self. Can you imagine all the ways you can transform your mundane activities into the most pleasurable experiences? Can you imagine it? We know you can. Self-fulfillment is no longer negotiable when you taste the freedom to be loved by life itself.

Chapter Six

Straddling Your Freedom

Those of you who are reading these words have come to a very important junction in your life. This junction has been faced by only a few humans in your past. You recognize its value and importance as simply being Spirit incarnate. Indeed, all of us, your family in Spirit that you left behind, are celebrating these times with you. For we recognize, as well, that it is important that you sense this celebration on your behalf. We recognize that the vast majority of humanity has yet to acknowledge your consciousness! We encourage you to attract relationships that are fulfilling to reinforce a personal reality that can feel very lonely at times. As you look out at the sea called humanity, we ask that you perceive with patience and compassion a consciousness that has yet to experience this place that you are at now.

We wish to share a perspective of a new challenge that is before each of you. For indeed, you have journeyed far to be at this place of new beginnings. And yet, there is this desire as well to bring into this new frontier much of what feels familiar. To that we wish to merge and blend our energies with another family, the family of Sananda. This family knows first hand the path that now lies before you. The one known as Jesus represented this family. He is not asking that you follow the same path, but he offers his guidance that serves to support and comfort each of you. Jesus came to this place in his life of having to choose how best to serve Spirit. For on the one hand, the desire to stay connected to his family, friends, and community was very strong, and yet, he too felt the presence of the Mother/Father energies in his life, and he knew he could not serve 'humanity' feeling torn by his human relationships. He made a choice—the seed of Spirit offered itself to be planted upon and within this planet. By doing so, he chose to be of service to the 'family of love' and to a future that would serve humanity. As he spoke, "I am thy Father," to many these were the words of a deluded human. And yet, the connection had been made within him, and no longer could he deny this presence. Here, in this now moment, he extends his heart to each of you as you ponder what he too experienced. Being of service to your past history, to the picture shown on your drivers license, will indeed be of great service for many, as many will feel a personal connection with you as they share their challenges, struggles, and concerns. Being of service to a sovereign consciousness that perceives all of life as being sacred, that is a very unique path.

We take this moment to bow before each of you and to catch our breath in awe and delight. For this is a path that Jesus walked, and each of you are coming to feel the weight of such a choice. You are discovering what served your life for so long does not resonate with these energies of Spirit. And yet, there is a sadness as if you are saying goodbye to a long time friend as you enter into a new experience that has not yet been defined for you or by you.

Being in the moment will create a separation between you and the collective consciousness of humanity. You have yearned, prayed, cried, and most joyfully demanded that Spirit come to you! But none of you knew of the resistance, the doubts, and the concerns you would encounter from your human nature. The resistance is futile! The love you have invoked and freely choose to embody does not fit within the parameters of a life that would ask that you compromise your magnificence. Love will feel stagnant in your personal relationships that are devoid of mutual affection, respect, and compassion. Love does not dance very well with work that leaves you feeling bored, discontented, or withdrawn. This love you have allowed to be your new life is your new identity. It is supported by thoughts that dwell on joyful experiences, ecstatic adventures, and promising futures. Like Jesus, you face the same choice.

We invite you to again breathe in the love we share with you. Let your minds settle into this moment. Our words are not intended to bring fear into your life but are laced with a perspective that we feel you are ready to contemplate and perhaps embrace. We feel in each of you a hesitation, a reluctance. You are beginning to consider saying goodbye to a life that you have known to make room for one you have yet to create. In part, the words that we and others share are intended to inspire you to feel the excitement and fulfillment of finally leaving a consciousness that is based on fear and separation. We ask that you welcome into your heart the joy of being in this wondrous moment and the opportunity to experience your self as Spirit!

All of you were born into this world with the opportunity to discover that duality is not the only reality. Each of you reading these words has chosen to believe and feel that there exists another reality that is not based on reflections. You have discovered various healing modalities that have served your healing process. You have uncovered the layers of wounds you inherited from the conditioned beliefs and behaviors of your collective consciousness. The pain of this separation was so great at times that many of you cried at night to return to our side and leave this tormented heart behind. And yet here you are, the ones who thrive on challenges facing perhaps your greatest challenge—to leave mass consciousness behind but remain here on earth.

We invite you to explore this opportunity before you, playfully imagining yourself at a crossroad. Here you stand looking at this fork that faces two roads going opposite directions. The road on the left has but one sign that reads: Spirit Road. All of you have felt the presence of this road as you allowed the energy of Spirit to come to you. There is a feeling of peace, bliss, and an overwhelming sense of joy! On this road, 'we' exist. Each step you take, you feel the veil thinning, and our energies merge, blend, and reconnect.

Those of you who have ventured a few steps down this road noticed there are no sign posts and there is no map to guide you. Shaking your head, you return to the crossroads to contemplate this road.

On the right is a sign that reads: Humanity's Past, and indeed, it could as well simply read a polarized life. Separation from Spirit/Joy. This road, however, comes complete with sign posts and maps all leading to fond memories, relationships, and current occupations. This road keeps you connected to your family members, parents, children, co-workers, and friends. On this road resides at this time 98% of humanity. They are not conscious that another road exists, and when you share of your discovery, you are seen as being out of touch with reality. Some of you have shared your experience of Spirit with many on this road. Humanity listens but reminds you that life is not about wishful thinking. You look at humanity feeling baffled by their reluctance to accept another reality, and they in turn remind you to start accepting reality.

On this road called Humanity's Past, they have forgotten to allow Spirit to come to them. They have forgotten that they too are Spirit. Their perception and experience of life is based on feeling disconnected from joy, passion, and trust. Their understanding of love is based on sacrifice and

100

compromise. The notion of loving yourself sounds vain and selfish. We would agree that the road of Spirit is indeed the road of adventure! The majority of humans on this road are not mean-spirited. They are generous and kind in their understanding of love. Many of you have found sincere relationships with others on this road, while some of you have found it to be unbearable. Now, we are not intending to pass judgment but rather to clarify a profound opportunity that is before each of you in this moment, for we feel your heart connections with this family of yours that seems trapped in a polarized, collective reality. You want to be of service to their journey in life, offering support in their struggles to be free at what ails them. And yet, as you have discovered yourself, a polarized duality only serves it's own reflection. To truly be of service to Spirit, we are asking you, "Where is your allegiance?"

We notice that the pulling of your heart strings has you straddling both roads, one foot in each reality. As you walk and become immersed in each road simultaneously, you begin to literally feel stretched, stressed, and eventually confused. You believe that those who reside on the road to the right will feel abandoned and rejected by you not maintaining a presence, both physically and emotionally. While straddling both roads, your body is giving you day-to-day reports on the state of its health. It is clearly stating how it is that you are trading one pain for another. So we are here to ask of you to reconsider how best to serve humanity and yourself at this time. We ask of you to experiment with putting both feet on the road of Spirit, spending longer periods of time feeling your strength and vitality return to you.

We are not asking that you leave your body or this planet. To the contrary, we are asking that you stay fully connected to your body while venturing down this new road. Some of you have ventured far enough to leave sign posts that read: Rest Stop. It is here that you can fully absorb the ecstasy of Spirit rejuvenating your body, mind, and emotions. You are making the signs as you go, and the majority of you will want to return to the crossroads to teach humanity about Spirit. We are suggesting that this crossroad is the meeting point that will serve your health and well-being. This crossroad will allow you to stay connected to Spirit and allow humanity to feel and recognize the 'love' that flows through you. You will not feel responsible for others, but you will freely respond to the needs and desires of humanity without depleting your energy.

On the road to the right, you learned that to love yourself was vain. Serving yourself was considered to be self-centered. This road to the left will ask of you to become very honest and sincere about the nature of sharing love. The road of Spirit will invite you to share the overflow of self-fulfilling experiences. We ask you to consider these words and experiment with consciously loving yourself on a daily basis. Put on your calendar dates and times that honor a new joy for life that respects an emerging self love.

You will discover that you can serve your family, friends, and co-workers without taking on their crisis by meeting them at the crossroad. This crossroad allows you to stay connected to Spirit and asks of them to take one step out of their known reality. For at this crossroad, they can hear and feel what you have to share. For many years to come, we see humanity simply learning to trust being with you at this crossroad. The majority, even from this vantage point, will not perceive the Spirit Road. That will come in time. In the meantime, straddling your freedom will exhaust and deplete your energies. Placing both feet on the road of passion, wisdom, and adventure allows you to serve in the capacity that Jesus served and beyond! You have discovered a grand new identity, and the realness of such love will be felt and seen by the example you are living.

You have come so far, and you are allowing yourself to taste but a morsel of Spirit in your life. There is a feast waiting for you! We challenge you to join us in this feast.

Step up to the front of the line and choose a diet that is ful-filling. Many of you are waiting for the next book or channel that will provide the missing piece to this puzzle called life. But we say to you, the book of a life based on Spirit is being written by you, reunited with us and lived as one. We shall adopt your diet of challenges by challenging you to let love be your 'new identity.' We are waiting with napkins in hand, relishing your arrival. Reunited on the road of Spirit, we can truly serve humanity in ways that never would have been possible. We love you all dearly and continue to serve you as you begin to serve LOVE as Self!

Chapter Seven

A Spiritual Architect

In your childhood, new experiences were presented to all of you on a daily basis. You developed new skills that left you feeling frustrated and overjoyed at the same time. Learning to walk was an art form of being in the moment. Each step sent ripples of excitement throughout your entire body. You felt like you had finally arrived, strutting your magnificence for all to see. It was not a piece of cake for any of you. It took a deliberate focus to trust that those small legs would support you. Every time you fell, you faced the same choice. Continue to crawl within the safe parameters of your known environment or trust in your ability to learn something new.

For most of you, it took several months to master walking as a child. Each day presented you with new challenges and more opportunities while your skills developed. As adults you take this huge leap of trust for granted. You simply know that walking is a natural state of being.

We continue to invite you to have new experiences. We know they will challenge the physical, emotional, and social parameters you have grown accustomed to. Your willingness to consider a non-dualistic relationship with life can and will feel like learning to walk all over again. It will demand of each of you to trust in your inherent ability to adapt to this new way of being. Learning to walk did not happen overnight, and we remind you that walking was but the beginning of discovering the flexibility, the strength, and the agility of your body. For those of you who are entering the later phase of your human existence, you are still discovering new attributes of these physical vessels.

As we introduce the concept of creating your own experience, we encourage each of you to draw from the wisdom you have already developed and from the skills you have already learned. It required patience, focus, humor, and a willful determination to master these skills.

Walking is an art form that you now practice everyday. You lose sight of your creative abilities when you take something so beautiful as walking for granted.

Within these pages, you will find numerous examples of ways to drastically alter your perception and your life. If you only store this information and this knowledge in your mind for safekeeping, then you are choosing to continue crawling within the safe parameters you have unsuccessfully tried adapting to. Walking into a non-polarized reality is a way of life that will reward you with every step you take. Keeping these new desires only in your mind is but playing with more concepts. Although that can led to some very stimulating conversations, in time, that too becomes boring. The fulfillment of human beings who have embodied their personal freedom is a result of their day-to-day devotion to walking the road of Spirit. In a way, becoming a spiritual architect will bring you back to your childhood. It is here that you freely used your imagination to create your experiences. It is within your imagination that you will discover your inherent ability to manifest your thoughts into physical reality. A physical reality that denies the natural extension of its nonphysical counterparts can indeed be very frustrating for it limits and confines you to a range of beliefs that deny you your birthright. You may have whatever your heart desires. That statement alone can be extremely frustrating if you attempt to honor that belief while feeling disconnected from your heart.

Many of you have attempted to change your exterior environment by opposing those who disagree with your beliefs. Confronting others was meant to strengthen your own beliefs, proving yourself to be right by making someone else wrong. The majority of humanity does not share your passion for embodying Spirit at this time. This gives you the freedom to explore a unified consciousness while sharing the same physical environment. You begin to accept that what others choose for themselves is truly none of your business. Now, many of you will suggest that if you turn a blind eye to all the injustice and corruption of this world, you are allowing that which is corrupt to spread. Does your history not give you evidence of your own fear? How do you feel when others insist that you must believe as they do? Again, do not take our words at face value. Put them to the test by withdrawing yourself from your external battles and heal the internal conflict within yourself. Remove your consciousness from engaging in polarized confrontations and witness the effect you have in your personal relationships with your friends, neighbors, and community. Put it to the test and see if indeed this is true.

Like learning to walk, choosing to embrace and embody your divine nature will become a day-to-day experience, each moment adding to the next. Over your life, you have proven your ability to adapt to your collective consciousness. You had to learn skills and develop abilities that truly challenged your integrity. In comparison, embodying Spirit only asks of you to embrace what has always been within your heart. You have already accomplished the most difficult task. What lies before you awakens abilities that are simply dormant.

There is a small minority of human beings who feel that mass consciousness is suffocating their heart's expression. They are the first wave of souls that have collectively shattered this cocoon of fear and are just beginning to test their new wings. We are speaking to these brave and courageous souls that have awakened from a dream that demands that you deny yourself your own freedom for the price of existing within the safe parameters of this cocoon. We are deeply honored to serve you by reminding you of how life itself wants to serve you.

Within the parameters of a polarized reality, you attempted to confine your magnificence to a set of beliefs that would suggest you are not worthy of God's love. We have been sharing that Spirit comes with no agenda, it offers to blend its presence with whatever choices you make for yourself. The frustration you feel comes from trying to activate this new relationship within a system of reality that has separated itself from Spirit. As we share some thoughts on how you can manifest your desires, we give you our promise that, with a little practice, you will experience the pleasure of life serving you.

You have learned that by working very hard, sacrificing your own needs, and compromising your feelings, you could eventually earn the abundance you desire. As you learn to unwind yourself from all the beliefs that have supported such a diminished experience, you open your life to the presence of Spirit. As you learn to accommodate this new relationship, you will experience what you have called in your past - miracles. These experiences require no effort on your part and perhaps that is why they seem so unreal. Why would life choose to serve you? It is because you and Spirit share the same lineage. You are beginning to fall in love with the perfection of who you are in this moment.

This book is enticing you to stop working so hard to receive so little. It is within this place that your mind will serve you very well by asking, "How exactly do we receive from life?" We have invited you to play with 'being in receivership.' Although very simple by design, this practice will dramatically shift the energy flow between you and the universe. As you become more skilled in maintaining a receivership mode, you will then be able to play with the art of consciously creating your own experience. A spiritual architect knows that a deliberate state of imagining life is a powerful place from which to manifest one's desires. You will learn to consciously play with your imagination, visiting imagined environments that you design to fit your needs. You begin to experience these imagined potentials as they trickle into your life. In your past, the energy field around your planet reflected the polarized inner relationship of humanity. This feeling of separation from love naturally manifested a collective force field that reflected the pain of love being withheld. In such an energy, it was almost impossible to experience the rewards of being in receivership. We share this simply to remind you that your grand photographer is lacking pictures of you being on the receiving end of a love without any agenda. It will attempt to serve you by suggesting that your imagination is just your imagination. Give it tangible proof of your power by dreaming of endless, fulfilling possibilities. Daydreaming is considered by many to be a distraction. It is time to recognize its value.

Creating your Sanctuary

Let us play with a potential environment for you to consider imagining. Take some time to bring yourself into a playful, open, and joyful feeling. We will warn you from the start that trying or efforting will backfire in this process. It is a state of receiving that allows life to come to you. We would like you to play with the idea of creating a sanctuary for yourself in the realm of your imagination. A place for you to visit anytime you wish to rejuvenate your body, quiet the mind, or restore a sense of well-being. Choose an environment that perhaps you have always dreamt of as a human. For many of you, you will choose to surround yourself with the majestic beauty of this earth, perhaps by the ocean, in the forests, the desert, or by a rambling stream. Choose any environment you desire and allow yourself to go deeply into the feeling of 'knowing' you de-serve and very much enjoy such a place.

Now, begin to imagine what type of sanctuary pleases you the most. Is it a temple, perhaps a lodge, or simply a tree house? Play with different designs and structures until you get a feeling for your preference. Now begin to imag-ine the shape and size of your preferred sanctuary. Be playful with this. It is not necessary to hold or visualize an image. It is more important that you have a sense of how

112

you feel in this place. Is there a path leading up to it? Is it sunny, raining, or snowing? Are there flowers blooming? How would you like the interior of your sanctuary to be decorated? Very serene or perhaps lavished with furniture, rugs and artwork. What colors do you prefer? How does it smell? Are there cookies always baking? Has the sweet smell of nature made its way into this sacred space? What type of windows do you prefer? What do you see when you are looking out? Now walk around and imagine touching the texture of everything you have placed inside. Let all of your senses feel the realness of this place. Take your time. Let your mind get a nice long look at your new environment.

Now, imagine a place or chair that is reserved for conscious creation. While sitting on this chair, a blank screen descends from the ceiling. This screen is your blank canvas for your imagined potentials. Let us play with this screen by referring to anything in your life that is now bringing or has brought you joy. Go for the most exhilarating experience you have ever tasted as a human. Let yourself soak in those feelings for a few minutes and then bring yourself back to sitting in front of this screen. Still feeling connected to your joyful memory, what would you like to now add to your life. Perhaps a new car, living arrangement, or a more fulfilling job. See yourself on the screen 'feeling' - yes, 'feeling' - very fulfilled sitting next to a new car, in front of a new home, or in a new job. The background image can be like a snap shot. The most important part is how you are feeling as you imagine such a possibility. See yourself jumping for joy, doing somersaults, or embracing others. When you notice the energy beginning to wane, that is your signal to now close your eyes, and imagine feeling these potentials coming from your sanctuary into your physical reality. Imagine these potentials coming into your body like falling raindrops. It is this simple!

Now, life will say yes to everything! Your only job to receive this gift is to consciously stay connected to being in receivership. Feeling loved by life becomes your new focus! We hear many of you saying to us that this takes a lot of work. Dear soul, you do not get exhausted from being in receivership. You adapted to a collective consciousness that placed your worth and value in the hands of others outside of you. And how is that going?

Being in receivership is a new way of life. It will take some practice, but we are certain that once you experience your exalted state of being, you will never go back to crawling again. Just as you have developed the art of walking, the art of being in receivership demands the same focus. By developing a conscious relationship of feeling life coming to you energetically, you will naturally find yourself in the moment without all the efforting. All that time which you have spent regurgitating your past and projecting it into your future did not allow for a conscious creation. That way of thinking became the only reality that truly exists, whether you were thinking about yesterday or wishing for tomorrow. It can now all happen in this moment, if you will allow yourself to also be in this moment. You will then notice that life truly wants to serve you. How will you know this? You will feel the presence of Spirit pouring down into your body, thoughts, and experiences.

And now we are back to the choice at hand. Will it be the pain and struggle of trying to get life to recognize your worth, or will you allow yourself to be loved just as you are? You are reading this book for you have questioned the very nature of reality. It is our joy to inspire you to experience for yourself the answers that lie within you. Waiting for the elixir to drip from the bosoms of creation, it is time to learn to be in receivership. It is time to stop teasing your mind with trickles of love when there is a continuous waterfall available to anyone who is willing to receive it. It is time to change the relationship within yourself so you can create a new collective relationship that is supported by Spirit.

It is a grand time to be on earth. This is your opportunity while sharing the same environment with the majority of humanity to free yourself from the grip of fear. You have adapted to the beliefs and conditions that have served your survival but left you spiritually depleted and exhausted. It is time to spread your new wings, learn to fly with your new expressions, and to discover who you have been all along.

Chapter Eight

Self-Betrayal

We have been exploring the parameters of your human nature by suggesting that you examine the conditions and beliefs you have inherited. You have also questioned the limitations of your past that asked you to compromise your sense of worth. We celebrate your failure to accommodate the polarization of your own consciousness but please understand that your human nature feels very confused and takes this failure personally. You did not incarnate into physical reality to simply accommodate the problems humanity faces without also offering a solution.

This solution that many of you are beginning to experience first hand comes to you when you stop listening to the thoughts that suggests you are not Spirit. If you truly were to trust that you no longer need humanity's permission to embody your own divinity, you would open your senses up to a profound and ecstatic relationship with your own divine nature. Many of you are feeling that you are betraying your relationship with your parents, friends, children, and your co-workers by shifting your allegiance. It is our service to each of you to mirror back to you how you are betraying your own magnificence, Spirit incarnate. Allowing Spirit to love you just as you are liberates your soul from its story, which impacts your soul family throughout all of creation.

Many throughout your history have explored the very dilemma each of you is now facing. They asked many of the same questions, "How do I live within this world and not be a part of it?" Many experienced the presence of Spirit in an altered state that was disconnected from their physical reality. They believed that the body was a hindrance in achieving an authentic relationship with Spirit. In this lifetime, many of you are discovering that the physical body is a beautiful biological receiver for any state of consciousness you are willing to merge with. Those in your past, who have also experienced this expanded self, struggled with integrating that presence into their day-to-day reality. Many found it to be impossible to maintain that connection and interact with the collective consciousness. They chose to live as hermits, shamans and healers, often within the heart of your forests, caves, and mountains. Many others created monasteries that offered a supportive environment, separate from the rest of the world, but available to those willing to devote their life to their understanding of Spirit.

In this lifetime, each of you has made a radical departure from these other types of living arrangements. You have discovered that your body can be your personal sanctuary. This new temple for Spirit is also mobile allowing you to explore the wonders of physical reality while maintaining your connection with your emerging self. Many of you have told us that you are able to share the same physical environment with the rest of humanity without compromising the true nature of your soul. We have enjoyed very much exploring with you the parameters of your human nature - your personality - by giving you the tools to work with this part of you that is a direct byproduct of those very parameters. You have learned that it is one thing to reject the restrictions of mass consciousness intellectually but quite another to embody a unified consciousness - a consciousness that does not dance with self-imposed limitations, or the denial of your own magnificence. This is where we find the majority of you at this moment. You are wanting to sincerely spread your angelic wings, but you are still feeling pulled by the influences you failed to adapt to. Once again, we must say congratulations on your failure! Perhaps now would be a good time for you to celebrate that. Now . . . now are you willing to devote the rest of your life to being the authentic ascended being you are right now? In your new life, there is a place for all of it - your personality, body, mind, heart, and soul. Unity consciousness is not about rejecting or opposing life. It embraces the sovereign reflection of your own perception, and changes that which does not reflect a love for self. The choice to embody such a consciousness is now available to each and every one of you. The pain and suffering is beginning to dwindle as each of you learns to become conscious of what you are thinking and how you are feeling.

Like many other nonphysical families, we have set the bar high, inviting you to taste the exquisite beauty of your own soul.

Many of you are beginning to discover latent, creative abilities that have been lying dormant for most of your life.

You have given yourself permission to explore these hidden talents even if you are the only one who has done so. Your personality, for most of your life, has been working overtime with its agenda to conform your identity to the very parameters you have adapted to but now reject. It has been seeking recognition from others for its service to you. Now is the time for your soul to assert itself and reassure the personality that life is safe and fulfilling outside the walls of your past. The sense of safety now comes not from shielding yourself from life but from developing a relationship with Spirit that will truly support your expressions. Being passive and indecisive are not the virtues of your authentic nature. There is a big difference between patience and procrastination.

When you choose to allow Spirit to support your expressions, you are actively seeding a new potential for your human family, a potential that allows your culture to embody sovereign principles as guidelines for your consciousness. This will take some time. More than your lifetime for there are many who now benefit from the separation between the heart, mind and Spirit. As each of you have already discovered for yourself, you cannot twist the arm of ignorance and expect it to receive love. We perceive over the next 200 years humanity opening its heart to this potential. From our perspective that is quite a quantum leap, and yet we know you were hoping it would happen sooner. It can happen in this lifetime for each of you individually. In fact, it must become an individual experience before it grows into a collective awareness. And again, we celebrate your inability to accommodate a reality that asks of you to continue feeling separate from your own true nature. You have already discovered that you simply cannot digest self-betrayal that denies that you are Spirit.

Now, betraying your true nature can be healed. This physical reality offers the perfect environment to practice sharing your own state of consciousness. You already know how that experience feels when you deny your own magnificence. Let us be very clear - you have not fallen from the stars. You can leave physical reality anytime you want. Nobody is holding you here for any reason. The only reason you are still here reading this book is to resolve your relationship with your own divine nature.

Here you are, living proof that love is real and ready to serve life. You are showing humanity tangible proof that, indeed, it is safe and extremely rewarding to trust in your heart's desires. Now is the time to give yourself whatever you have denied yourself. Humanity is waiting for someone to show them what Spirit and joy look like as a human being. Our brother, Jesus, spoke of a second coming, a time when a group of souls would descend into this reality and offer itself as Spirit. Now is that time, and each of you carries within you the very seeds of Christ consciousness. It is not a time for being passive. It is your time to become conscious of your own inner dialog and to choose how it is that 'you' want to feel. How do you want to feel? Can you risk feeling ecstatic waves of bliss supporting your life? These very waves, so to speak, deliver the 'second coming' to earth. Are you willing to be fulfilled, allowing joy to be your natural expression? Does this sound like a burden to you? No? Then walk out of the fear based cocoon that represents mass consciousness. This is the time for the butterflies to show their wings. Left in the cocoon, your Spirit will fester and rot in a polarized web.

It is time to feel the presence of Spirit, it exists outside of this cocoon that has imprisoned your soul. Practice throughout your day simply being in silence, breathing in each moment, one breath at a time. Without the need to define or describe your reality, a fresh new feeling will emerge. You will experience being at peace with yourself. As you allow this new feeling to be more and more a part of your life, your choices will begin to shift to accommodate this inner peace. It is not a passive state but a very dynamic one. It is Spirit, supporting you outside of the parameters you inherited. It is the real you, before your human mind begins to describe your identity. The describer, your mind, and the indescribable, your heart, are reuniting within the flesh of your human experience. It is a marriage that is a long time in coming, and you, dear souls, are the ones to allow such a grand reunion within yourself.

Denying your feelings makes the transition into joy a little more difficult. Acknowledging the truth of your own emotional resonance will serve you very well. You inherited many core beliefs that no longer serve your life, including your belief about being human. Some of your spiritual teachings have suggested that you betrayed God somewhere along the way or else you would not be here. They suggest that earth represents itself as a galactic penal colony that cuts you off from God's blessings until you demonstrate that you deserve 'his' love. This is a very interesting concept. The energy around and on your planet is thick with this belief that you have betrayed God. Without pointing fingers, who would benefit from such a marketing scheme, and who ends up feeling out of the loop of God's grace? Your soul is equal in worth in the eyes of Spirit to anything else in all of creation. Let us start with that premise and work our way out of this maze that would have you walking in circles.

Looking into your mirrors, you have the opportunity to walk away from the polarized nature of your world by declaring yourself to be beautiful. How long and how often are you willing to stare at yourself in awe of your inherent worth. This simple but powerful exercise will develop a sincere feeling that you are indeed lovable. In fact, you are perfect just as you are at this moment. You already know how it feels to betray your own beauty by denying yourself love.

Spirit doesn't need to be loved by others to feel love for itself. Its joy, however, resides in the sharing of this unconditional love for all of life. Each time you betray your own worth, you taste the futility of trying to meet the expectations of others. When you look into the mirror, you see reflected back the beauty and pain of your human experience. For most of your life, you endured great pain and accepted a belief that life will not support your heart's desires. You attempted to use your parents, siblings, children, friends, wives, husbands, co-workers, and employers as the source of your own sense of worth.

Self-love, to be authentic, simply asks each of you: "What do you want? How do 'you' want to receive love?"

Experiment with this. One of the ways we have suggested is to create 'joy dates' for yourself, giving yourself permission to have life give you what you desire. In your personal relationships, intimacy invites you to openly communicate how you like to be loved. How do you like to be touched? How many ways are you willing to experiment with allowing yourself to be pleasured? Experiment by yourself, and by asking others to pleasure you exactly the way you want to experience a new love for yourself. Letting life pleasure you because you ask for it will feel very vain. Congratulations! Loving yourself throughout your day will give you tangible evidence that you are beautiful. How? Go look in the mirror and see for yourself what emerges when you act on your own behalf.

As you grow comfortable with loving yourself, you will develop discernment in your personal relationships. By embracing self-love, you cannot become the missing piece in someone else's life. You cannot fill another person's void for them. In your intimate relationships, you openly share the relationship you have with yourself and relish the opportunity to share a love with each other that respects the sovereign nature of life.

You will find that many of your current relationships will go through many changes as you begin to embrace your own divine nature. You will learn to value yourself in a way that does not allow self-betrayal. This is an awkward time for many of you, for you have betrayed your own worth to support many of your personal relationships. Your heart will be pulled in many directions when you claim your own sovereignty. Asking the mirror to love you first before you trust that you are lovable is insane. Such is humanity's dilemma at this time. What will they see when they look into your eyes, dear reader?

Will you allow them to see that you have fallen in love with you? Will they see that you have made peace with your own divinity? Will you allow the suffering human to get a glimpse of the ecstatic nature of Spirit? Will you deny them the very elixir to their own internal suffering? Self-love!

Yes, we can now make a profound shift from the entangled patterns of behavior that would deny you the truth of your soul nature. Self-love allows the embodiment of Spirit, which in turn allows you to perceive that very presence in all forms of life. When Spirit is not allowed to be a part of your experience, the mind dutifully describes each form as being separate from itself. The united heart and mind can perceive that all of life is interconnected and that each soul has the freedom to be sovereign, choosing to blend and merge with any relationship it desires.

You experience this freedom by embracing your divine nature. By spending less time being critical of your own physical beauty and using humanity as a reference for what qualifies as being beautiful. As you begin feeding your body with the energy of new and uplifting thoughts, your body will respond with health and vitality. Your body, without all of your efforts to change it, will respond quite naturally to self-love. When you stop relying on the reflections of others as your source for happiness, you no longer play the game of being the victim. It is a very, very powerful stance to take.

During this time on earth, many of you have become familiar with the term 'equal opportunities.' We know the intent for such a title is meant to address discrimination. We commend humanity for taking such a stand and invite each of you to begin to use that term as a means to liberate the deeper reflection of your own self-discrimination which denies all aspects of your consciousness the right to express themselves. We find it very interesting how humanity chose to relate to the liberation of the female gender. Again, we congratulate the wisdom to address this very issue but find it amusing that you have placed the responsibility for liberating the female within by becoming more mindful or male-like.

Self-discrimination begins when you deny the full expression of both your heart and your mind. When you put the burden of liberating your female nature upon your mind, you are, again, asking the reflection to love you first. You expect the mind to fulfill for you what it can never accomplish. And yet, its devotion to you, soul, is so sincere that it will spend eons of time trying to figure out how does one liberate the female. It will pursue numerous agendas, chase endless dreams, and travel to great lengths only to discover that she is not 'out there.' She is not in the better paying jobs, but she will celebrate your willingness to receive your true worth. She is not in the playing fields of your athletes, but she will marvel at your willingness to explore the magnificence of your body's abilities. She is not in the armed forces, but she is willing to commend your determination to confront your fears.

Your self-discrimination as a human being now solely rests on the shoulders of your soul. It now asks of you, soul, to stop discriminating against physical reality as not being worthy of your full attention. It asks of you to fully embody and develop a healthy relationship with the one that has felt responsible for your life. The personality and your mind can now feel the presence of your female nature, and they ask you, soul, to guide them into this new relationship, lifting the burden from your male nature to liberate the sacred feminine. She was never trapped, but to know her, all of you have to learn to allow her presence to be in your life.

Discriminating against the Heart and Mind of Creation denies you the ability to love yourself. You are your body, mind/male, heart/female, and Spirit. Your history documents the futility in opposing and confronting life's reflection. Trying to change the world does not change you. If it could, then war would be celebrated as your greatest achievement. Changing you changes life, and it offers something original for all to reflect upon. We are calling for the new teachers to come forward to embody the presence of Spirit, which embraces all aspects of life.

When you acknowledge and validate what you have inherited, the denial loses its grip. You have every right to feel frustrated, angry and outraged, for you know in your heart what you compromised to fit into this collective dream. We are here to acknowledge that - yes, it is tarnished, but with a little practice you can return it to its original value - Self-love!

We are most honored to have this opportunity to be so direct and honest with you, dear reader. We know who our audience is. We have the deepest respect for those who are just beginning to awaken to a new relationship with Spirit and to those who have already embraced such a choice. History will proclaim how you failed miserably in your attempt to accommodate a polarized, dualistic system by igniting a passion for a galactic reunion within Spirit. You have invited Spirit, the sacred feminine and the divine mind to now be present on earth. Spirit will support your dreams and your visions, but you in turn, must support the presence of Spirit. How many ways have you loved yourself today? Feel the presence, nurture that relationship, and begin to express a new passion for living. The new teachers and healers demonstrate the sovereign and unique relationship you have embodied within yourself. Let humanity see in your eyes the truth of Spirit looking back, filled with compassion, acceptance and a profound love for life.

Chapter Nine

Circles of Support

As the winds of change continue to sweep into every facet of life on Earth, I, Archangel Michael, stand before you as a friend, teacher, and servant to a unified field of consciousness that supports all of creation. If you allow it, you can feel my presence touching your heart, reminding you that now is the time to reveal the gift you carry. This gift has been called by many names, and today we will call it the "seeds of change."

Seeds of Change

Before you incarnated, you knew that the soil or conditions on Earth could not support this sacred gift. You knew you would need to change the unfertile conditions to ensure that these seeds could grow. Many before you also attempted to plant these same seeds. Their attempts were honored, but the seeds, for the most part, never received the nutrients or energy they required. Despite all of this, each of you came again to this planet as bearers of the seeds of change, and much to your surprise these seeds have taken to Earth. Their roots have descended into a rich bed of nutrients that are now supported by a renewed human spirit.

As caretakers for these seeds, many of you spent several decades refining your relationship or connection with Spirit. You understood at a deep level that these seeds can only be activated by your love. You explored the nature of your wounded heart, your conditioned human nature by practicing a variety of different healing modalities. Many of you also began to experience a type of addiction to this healing process. You created a belief that the messenger or seed bearer must heal all of your human conditions in order to serve this sacred gift with integrity and honor. During this process, many of you also discovered a profound new relationship with your soul, but you choose to contain that experience to your own life. You embodied a type of unexpressed enlightenment.

All of you are deeply honored for being here. I, Michael, gave my word to each of you that I would remind you at times of the sacred nature of the gift you carry. It is a gift that every soul carries, but very few serve. There is now a small but vibrant group of humans who have walked out of their healing process and discovered a new sense of empowerment that utilizes many new creative abilities. They have consciously planted these sacred seeds within their own creative expressions. For some it has taken the form of a service. For others they choose to express this gift within a product. They are beginning to celebrate their own unique, artistic expression. They are discovering the more they share this gift, the more connected they feel to life and to an ongoing stream of support. They have embraced a new relationship to service that compliments their own sense of empowerment and abundance. Their creations are now beginning to take on a life of their own, drawing on additional resources and people for support. We celebrate this new awareness and remind all of you that this is just the beginning. Buckle your seat belts, you're going to enjoy this ride!

Shifting the Collective

These potent new seeds of change have developed their own unique root system. They are supported and interconnected within a series of other sacred seeds that have also sprouted. This in turn is shifting the energetic balance within the very core of your planet. For Gaia must accommodate whatever system of reality you embrace. Gaia is now accommodating a state of consciousness that is new, profound, and life altering within and above her crust.

For those who have become actively involved with serving these seeds of change, we notice many of you now perceive life from a radically different perspective. You recognize that your service to self was indeed an essential part of your growth. In hindsight, you see the value of your healing process for it uncovered many illusions. You became aware of a lingering cloud of inertia that hovered above your life for many years, attempting to deny your freedom of expression. This inertia kept the focus on you. It served to maintain an identity that was all about "me, me, me". You had become victims of your own healing process.

We share this perspective with you for in your horizon is another, much larger group of souls. They are indeed living on Earth and are just becoming conscious of these sacred seeds. We see this group numbering in the millions, they are feeling this urge to change with a lot of unanswered questions? They are just beginning to turn their attention away from a support system that no longer lives up to what was advertised. They are beginning to recognize your unique, creative expressions in a variety of services and products they hadn't noticed before.

Now, the timing of this shift is beautiful. Many of you have waited your whole life for this moment. You also became bored and disgruntled with the timing of this change. What is the point of serving change if no one is listening? We hear you and honor your patience. We now call out to those of you that are hiding in stale relationships, boring jobs and tired bodies. Seed bearer, now is the time! Where is your passion? When will you express it?

Serving Life

I, Michael, promised each of you that I would do whatever I could to remind you of your service to these sacred seeds. I ask of you again, who are you serving? For the mind will attempt to convince you that life doesn't need your passion. It doesn't need your joy. The mind will try to convince you that your fragile self esteem will only feel humiliated if you risk exposing your heart's desires. There is also this small yet vibrant group of humans who are now consciously serving life, waiting for you to join the party. Inviting you to share your creative gifts for all of humanity to see.

136

We will say it again; the family called humanity is just beginning to awaken from their own nightmare. This awakening process will continue for the next 200 years before it becomes your new collective consciousness. You are not here to stand on a pulpit declaring the truth of some God. Your creations will carry your message, infused by the presence of Spirit. They must however be visible to the human eye. Your human family will be looking for an authentic representation of a unified field of consciousness. How important is this? Let me be very clear....it is "required" at this time! Required if change is indeed what you serve! If a new consciousness is what you are truly celebrating!

I do not come on this day to give you weather reports of things to come. You can feel what is coming! I come to you to honor your service to life by addressing this cloud of inertia. Invite me or Yeshua into your life. We are very skilled at helping to ignite a new passion that places the "me" in the back seat. The new consciousness is about "we," and we are here to compliment your new desires.

Life is calling each of you to step out of your comfort zone not because we are trying to put you in harm's way. Dear soul, listen to us . . . you are in this moment in harm's way if your not serving your creative abilities. These seeds of change will not germinate if they are planted by the mind. The mind hasn't a clue what to do with them. It is time for your mind to begin serving the change! Stop teasing this family called humanity by denying them tangible evidence that life is truly sacred. Life or Spirit wants more than anything to serve itself as YOU. The new service is your passion in action. It is time to join the party and let the creations begin.

Chapter Ten

Living Alongside
Closed Systems of Reality

There is no greater joy in all of creation than to experience a love that is freely shared without any conditions, agenda or expectation. Such a love has all but been forgotten on Earth, and yet something stirs within your heart to remind you of its existence. Every human being has the potential to rediscover this love - to reawaken a passion that is soul based - to reunite your human identity with the immense presence of your divine nature. Throughout the history of the human species, many have wondered, some have questioned, but very few have embodied such a presence - not because you didn't deserve it, but something else within the identity of every human does not trust such a love.

These times represent such a magnificent shift from a human story which would deny you the pleasures of life, deny you the abundance that you deserve, deny you your birthright to be free. This lifetime offered a profound choice for the family of humanity. Would humanity choose to live out their lives within the last chapter of this story or stop relying on this very old story and start creating a new life?

Closed Systems of Reality

Prior to this incarnation on Earth, each of you sat in a type of soul council meeting with many angelic beings. We shared our perspective of the choices that humanity would face. We talked of the grand galactic cycles that exist within all of creation. We reflected on the nature of these cycles, the beginning or birthing stage, the potential for expansion and growth and /or a completion stage. These cycles honor the eternal gift that was given to every soul. It was a gift that embraced change, growth, and expansion as being a natural part of life. These cycles allow Spirit to participate within its own creation. There also exist systems of reality that deny Spirit access.

We sat together prior to this lifetime knowing that Earth was a part of a grand, 26,000 year cycle that was about to enter the stage of completion. It appeared to all of us in the non-physical realms that humanity lacked the passion or clarity to embrace life as being sacred. Humanities future was uncertain, would they allow this cycle to expand into another phase of existence. It appeared that life on Earth would not continue as you know it to be today. Humanities future looked bleak and yet each of you incarnated to serve a new choice. You embraced the opportunity to experience a sovereign identity within a closed system of reality.

Now, within any system that is being controlled, it appears within that reality that the control is being imposed from the outside. Human beings continue to point fingers at those that they believe are denying them what they deserve to receive. Prior to this incarnation, each of you could clearly perceive the source of this control. Despite this, you agreed to participate knowing that the very nature of such a reality would attempt to deny you access to your own soul nature. Each of you understood that during the course of your life there was no assurance you would remember or experience the presence of Spirit. Those of us that stayed behind agreed to do everything in our power to remind you of why you are here. You accepted the conditions of life on Earth and still chose to be here.

The potential for change was very, very small. Humanity would need to once again value life in a way that would allow consciousness to coexist within this closed system of reality. Such a choice would free humanity from the endless cycles of oppression, injustice and denial.

As we speak of Earth, do you recall the thick, clouds of despair that circled around this planet? Do you recall the few points of light that acted as portals for love to enter? As we looked at this planet, you could clearly see it wasn't a group of ET's controlling life on Earth. It wasn't any particular government, religious organization, corporate entity or military power controlling life on Earth. They all played a part of course, but none of these were the source of the control. It wasn't any race of beings, a certain gender, or a particular culture. As we sat together in soul council, you saw consciousness or Spirit was being denied access to its own creation by the human mind.

The mind, living outside of the presence of an unconditional love, sought recognition outside of itself. The story of the human mind is supported by its need for power, conquest, and control, and of course it doesn't like to be reminded of the reality it has created. The human mind quickly denies the part it played in creating all of the suffering, injustices, and betrayals. It is a creator that has yet to learn to take responsibility for its own creations, for it fears of being judged as harshly as it judges itself. The human mind has long forgotten the attributes of the divine mind. Until NOW!

The New Souls

I, Michael, speak to you now while sitting in council with another group of souls. Like you, these souls have chosen to incarnate as a human being. Unlike you, many of these souls have never tasted physical reality. The only reason they are considering this opportunity is because of you. Your willingness to examine the mind's control has inspired them to look at Earth. You have demonstrated that opposites can coexist. We know this hasn't been easy or comfortable, and it certainly is not for the faint of heart. You have modeled, in your own unique way, how to resolve a polarized, dualistic relationship that impacts all of life.

Your devotion is truly rare! Your ability to trust in the unknown qualities of your own consciousness is almost unheard of, and you still wonder why we insist on kissing your feet. You accomplished the unimaginable! Despite all the conditions you inherited, you turned to your conditioned mind, acknowledged its control issues, and began a profound healing process.

As I, Michael, sit in council with these new souls, we are witnessing a planet that is very different from the planet you saw. The energy around Earth is no longer closed or contained. The grand, galactic cycle that appeared to be ending has shifted into an expansive mode. It appears to us that you simply opened the window, let life in, and now you can breathe again. Like a breath of fresh air, new possibilities are now springing up everywhere. As you breathe this new life into your body, you begin to imagine new possibilities for yourself. New insights replace the lack of hope and despair that was suffocating your Spirit.

New Appetite

You patiently taught your mind how to be in receivership. For most of you this was introduced as a healing practice. The intention was to open a door within your heart that would allow consciousness to once again participate in this reality. As you learned to trust in your receiving abilities, your mind began to experience the overwhelming presence of an unconditional love. Your mind experienced a love that acknowledged the reality of this closed system without judgment, with compassion, and with a solution for every problem the mind had created. With consciousness or Spirit now in your life, the old story has nothing to feed on. Old habits could not fulfill new dreams. As you trusted more and more in the mysterious presence of consciousness, you discovered a new appetite for living. You discovered a sincere joy that was having its way with you in every aspect of your life.

Now, each moment represents a choice to be free or to allow your mind to dictate what choices should be considered. Many of you have already made that choice and have been practicing staying connected to the moment with a newfound devotion. You discovered from this simple practice that consciousness or Spirit only exists in the moment. Some of you are beginning to reap the benefits from allowing this grand reunion which embraces a relationship with this conditioned aspect of your human nature. It is this internal work, practiced and enjoyed by millions that has also expanded out into all aspects of life on Earth. Indeed, the future for closed systems of reality continues to look bleak. During this lifetime, you can live alongside these systems of control without living within them. Many of you now have all the tools you need to shift your allegiance with this new partner called Spirit.

Your New Partner

Spirit doesn't play by the same rules the mind invented. It feels awkward initially to surrender the mind's control and to allow your creative abilities to be expressed in a graceful, joyful, and compassionate manner. Consciousness knows itself as being the source of life. Your newfound confidence in your ability to manifest what your heart desires now has a foundation to support it. Because of you, this grand cycle that repeats itself every 26,000

145

years is now entering into a stage of expansion. We celebrate this change with you for it allows trapped energies to be released within your body, this planet and your galaxy.

Soul Council Circles

I, Michael, now sit with some of the very same souls that sat with me prior to this incarnation, but now we meet in council here on Earth. These new soul council circles offer a safe and sacred place to give voice to your own consciousness - to hear the sounds of your own wisdom and truth resonating within every cell of your body. To encourage and support all who attend and to acknowledge, without judgment or shame, how challenging it can be to live alongside your conditioned mind. Sharing how confusing it can be when the mind attempts to filter and manipulate your truth. In these soul council groups here on Earth, you have also chosen to model this imperfect relationship between complete opposites as being the new human. As I share my presence with these new groups, I am deeply touched by the courage and trust in a presence that has been denied for so long. In these new soul council circles I, Michael, honor the souls who opened the windows on Earth and allowed life to once again serve you. We, your angelic family have come rushing in to reunite with our friends who choose to serve love. We invite all of you to create your own support groups! Celebrate your freedom with your voice! In the safety of these circles, you will learn to trust in the voice of your own soul nature. As that voice becomes familiar, you will begin to share not only the energy but the words that follow the energy in all of your relationships.

A New Relationship

I can now serve you in a new way. Humanity still calls out to the legions of angels under my guidance, asking that we provide for them what they lack within themselves. It was a role we agreed to play within this closed system of reality. Now that you have opened the windows, you truly don't need me to be your angelic bodyguard. There are countless bridges you will cross in your life that will eventually lead you back to yourself. Each bridge within this closed system will entice you with a variety of spiritual toys that will indeed entertain the mind. Your heart has no passion for playing games, it becomes bored and restless with all the ways you pretend not to be a creator of your own experience. It acts as a sacred portal for your own magnificence. The presence of consciousness, the source of life, changes everything. Embrace me dear human as your equal, one who enjoys serving the new creators of life. How may I serve you?

Together, we now face a human family that is just beginning to question their reality within this closed system. There will be a lot of finger pointing, but eventually they must face the same dilemma each of you experienced. The control begins from within and from within is where the change must begin. You have prayed, meditated, and demanded that the presence of Spirit make itself known on Earth. Now that your mind is so exhausted from resisting, you can feel your life being touched by love once again. Remember dear souls, Spirit will not force itself upon anyone, you must be willing to receive this partnership.

The vast majority of humanity has yet to experience Spirit in a direct, tangible manner. You now serve your human family by representing this new relationship. I have carried the sword of truth for a very long time. I lay my sword down in honor of the peaceful warriors that I may use both of my hands to embrace you! My love for each of you, without exception, is eternal.

Chapter Eleven

Questions and Answers • Part One

Question: It seems to be a part of our human nature to always resist change. Is there the potential that humanity will enter into this new paradigm gracefully?

Michael: (Michael laughs) Yes, the potential always exists! We would say the collective experience, as it is being acted upon now, is one of the more graceful choices available to all of you. Indeed, your human family is very addicted to all the drama/trauma that is connected to life altering changes. We know that for many of you it is very uncomfortable to live alongside a family that fears change. Many on our side of the veil have been sharing with you a

149

variety of spiritual tools and practices that serve to empower your own sovereign nature. It is very easy to get pulled into these dramatic responses to change on many levels. We deeply respect and understand the challenges you face everyday. In general, those that allow their own hearts to guide their life will find these changes will also enhance all that their heart's desire. Trusting your own inner guidance and owning your capacity to choose how "you" want to experience life will enhance the joy and wonder of being in the middle of all these changes.

The vast majority of humanity still allows others to define their life for them. Various organizations profit from this relationship and use fear to promote their agenda. They will insist that the future of life on Earth is in peril. This is not the time for any of you to play follow the leader and yet many lack the awareness or conviction to change this type of behavior. Those of you that are extremely sensitive to these collective inner conflicts will consider taking a sabbatical from planet Earth. There is no judgment or shame in this choice. Your service to life continues no matter what environment you choose for yourself. For those of you that subscribe to a heaven on Earth type of scenario, one that only embraces the light, you might be in for a rough ride. We have been saying for many years that this transition will unfold over many generations out of compassion and with grace. That doesn't mean any of you need to wait to embody that experience for yourself. Each of you act as a bridge between the angelic realms and your physical reality. Your ability and willingness to maintain that connection is a blessing beyond measure. It will take a little.....um, it will take a lot of patience to allow your human family to wake up from their own nightmare. Earth is a place for any being to resolve what they feel they are lacking in their relationship to their own divinity. Many will discover a type of self love that has been missing from your world. Will a heaven on Earth also allow for the conflicts, disagreements or even wars to also coexist? You might be surprised.

Question: Has the baby boomer generation fulfilled its mission?

Michael: If by that you mean did your generation contribute to the shift in humanities' consciousness, then indeed it has fulfilled its service very well! You have heard many times that you volunteered to be a part of this human experience to model another choice for your human family - a choice that would be based in love. Humanity did indeed respond to your presence, and like many of you, they now face the task of allowing that choice to become a conscious part of their day-to-day reality. What we find extraordinary about many in your generation is your desire to continue to serve this transformation even after you fulfilled your initial service. Let's be clear about this new choice. Your service is now to yourself. It involves allowing the immense presence of your magnificent nature to also participate in your physical reality. This new service is supported by your willingness to love your life just as it is at this moment. It is indeed a service that is based on self love. A love that does not compromise its own value or worth for the sake of others.

Question: I have a question for Yeshua, how much of the Bible actually reflects the real story of your life as Jesus? **Yeshua**: Ah! You live in a time when information is freely shared, directly from its source. Imagine your world today if only I had a laptop! Any of you can share your own thoughts using your words to describe "your" experience. The truth of my life continues to live inside your own heart. The conditioned human mind attempts to distort that truth as others have done in the past. The human experience is full of complex interactions that involves the mind, body, ego, collective consciousness and aspects of your soul. Most of humanity would be hard pressed to know the truth of what they experienced last week let alone the truth of another person. My story is no more important than your own. The truth of my life as Jesus was much like your own. At times my human nature allowed the voice of Yeshua and the Family of Sananda to express itself. That expression is indeed profound. It is available to all of you! Most of you reading these words have grown to embrace the energy of your soul, and, like me, your human nature also wants to declare itself to be your true identity. This represents a grand galactic story, told over and over again of how your soul experiences itself as being separate yet also a part of All That Is. Serve your own life, be true to your own heart. If you want to serve my story with all your heart, set it free, and embrace your own.

Question: Those of us that have embraced these changes seem to be dealing with a lot of health issues. How would you suggest we relate to these?

Michael: There are now intense eruptions of energy occurring within the collective consciousness of humanity and within the Earth. They are all a part of this process of moving energies that do not serve self love. In the past you could store your issues and feelings deep within your own body. There, they would fester and rarely reach the surface of your conscious awareness. Now there is an openness to acknowledge and heal these wounds with a newfound love for life. Many of you have already gone through this healing process but deny yourself the gift of being healed.

You see how difficult this transition is for others and continue to run their issues through your body. We

153

believe this type of compassion is misplaced for you are also denying your human family the benefits and rewards you experienced yourself in your own healing process. Your service now will look vain and will leave many of you feeling selfish for embracing, without guilt, your own health and well being.

We have spoken of how life truly serves whatever choice you make for yourself. Your current state of being is a beautiful reflection of this profound freedom. Continue to breathe in the gift you gave to yourself - JOY with every breathe you take, no matter what you are feeling. It is a choice and only you can make it for yourself.

Question: Will the worldwide economy survive these changes?

Michael: The worldwide economy is just beginning to align itself with the nature of consciousness or Spirit. It will appear to many that your economy is falling apart. It is in a dramatic transtion that now demands that your products and services value the sacredness of all life. Have you noticed how easy it is to fall into the new mantra that suggests these are tough times for everyone? We are not trying to undermine that. For many this transition will be very difficult. At the same time, we ask all of you to remember your capacity to create for yourself whatever experience you desire, no matter what others are choosing.

Our question to each of you is very simple. Will you allow joy to guide your choices?

Question: Thank you for the overview, but I was hoping for more details. Can you talk about the housing market, job opportunities, and the future of corporate identities?
Michael: Indeed! Our joy is to serve your soul by acting as a mediator with your human nature. We can speculate on any number of possibilities, but for those potentials to exist or at least be recognized each of you must first recognize who is guiding your own life. Your market is adjusting not failing. Not all aspects of it will survive these changes while others will thrive. Is this a good time to purchase real estate - relative to what? The value of property 5,10 or 15 years ago? If it brings you joy, buy that new home. Your world economy is shifting from perceiving Earth and all life upon it as a commodity. A new world community is emerging and with it new jobs will be created. We have a new job for you. Stop listening to the news for 30 days and observe how your own creative abilities begin to awaken. Notice in your own life what choices you are willing to make that accommodate these new passions. There is a profound sense of joy waiting for you to claim it that will never make the evening news, but it will impact the world at large.

Question: Michael, so many lightworkers seem to have money issues. As hard as we try, many of us never seem to enjoy the freedom that money can provide. Can you share your perspective on this issue?

Michael: Indeed! We offered a message last year titled "The Gift of Creation" and asked our partner (Robert) to also include this message in our latest book (Living Inside your Passion). We used the analogy that in the old energy system, your body represented a singular experience of yourself.

The conditions you inherited from your early childhood stayed with you throughout your whole lifetime. You now live in an energy that is multi-faceted. Your body is now adjusting to a new energy that allows you to experience a more expansive version of your soul. In this new relationship, we used the analogy that your body now feels like a hotel. You now have access to many guests or aspects of your own soul, including your divine nature. Some of the guests living inside this hotel are very comfortable with money. Perhaps they experienced life on Earth surrounded by royalty.

Many of you have attempted to change your relationship to money by trying to change your current conditioning. This is a valid intention and perhaps the most familiar method of transformation. It is also the most difficult. The new path of least resistance invites each of you to begin to acknowledge these guests in your hotel. Many already embody the skills you lack and are willing to blend their presence with your human experience, co-creating whatever you desire.

Now - for this to become a tangible experience we return to the art of being in receivership. Being in receivership allows you to receive the energetic, non-physical templates for the physical experiences you desire. We have suggested that you practice breathing life into your body, create a vertical connection with source energy and imagine standing under a shower of life or simply feel all the energy around you that is freely shared by Gaia. The art of being in receivership takes practice and for it to become effective it also becomes a way of life.

Abundance doesn't just happen to you, you create it for yourself by taking responsibility for what you want and becoming conscious of feeling the energy of your desires. We notice many of you are willing to embrace the concept but avoid the practice. This is a co-creative process that involves a type of surrender on your minds part that would allow other aspects of yourself to enhance your experience.

The simplicity of being in receivership troubles your mind and triggers the addiction to playing the victim. It is a choice that will change your life and has the capacity to enhance all of your experiences with unlimited resources. Such a freedom isn't earned, all you need to do is to receive it.

Question: Michael, you seem to be the source for a lot of channels, how do we discern which one represents your truth?

Michael: My expression is not limited to one truth, it is multi-faceted. I offer myself to "blend" with any sentient being who desires to share their experience with me. There is no human being who completely embodies my presence, it is not my intention to override your human nature. It is my joy to serve both your personality and soul to coexist within these spectacular physical bodies. Those that allow me to speak with or through their own human identity, for the most part, also have a strong, personal connection to the Family of Michael. The messages can and will be very unique, as are the many aspects of your own consciousness. There is however a common element or energy signature that is present in every Michael channel. The energy of my presence radiates a universal love for all of life. At the core of my being, I too channel for source energy – the fire of creation. While listening to any channel, feel for the presence of this universal love. If the connection isn't being controlled or manipulated by your human personality, the words, for the most part will reflect that relationship.

Question: You have stated that you and your legion of angels are with us all the time. Doesn't it get boring watching us do the same things over and over again?

Michael: (Michael laughs) Consider this, would you find it boring to lack the choice to do otherwise? Perhaps the angels are so enamored with your ability to freely choose! I would not describe my time with any of you as being boring, you keep me very, very busy. It is your broken heart that is the most disturbing to all of the angels and it is why we continue to share our compassion for your human condition. You see, we know you are simply pretending not to be creators, and if that is your choice God/Goddesses/All That Is - that is what we serve.

Question: I love to feel your presence in my life and want to thank you for all that you do. I have been attending some of your workshops and still find it hard to accept that I too am channeling for you. Can you help me get over this feeling that I'm just making it all up?

Michael: Indeed! The good news is I am more than happy to help you. The bad news is that you truly are making all of your life up as you go. There is a part of you however that believes it can freeze time, create a static identity, and pretend all is well.

I, Michael am not looking for another human channel, I am encouraging all of you to channel for your own truth as you connect to the deepest parts of your own soul. In the process you might discover that your soul is also deeply connected to the energy you call Michael. All of us are aspects of source energy or God and have are own individual and multi-faceted identities.

As you deepen your connection with your soul and develop a stronger sense of trust in the unknown, you will also develop a profound compassion for a mind that keeps telling you that none of this is real. Your species has a tendency to undermine new discoveries that contradict your known reality. Imagine your world today without electricity, telephones, airplanes or computers. Discovering your ability to communicate for your own divinity, using whatever name you want to call it including your own, is currently a new discovery for your species. It is natural to second guess yourself when you are the inventor. Keep practicing, I am happy to serve as a mediator between you and your soul.

Question: Yeshua, will you incarnate again during my lifetime?

Yeshua: If you are asking, will I repeat the same birthing process I experienced as Jesus, that is still unknown. You see, the second coming of Christ consciousness is all about

YOU! Will you allow the Christ to incarnate into your life representing itself as YOU? I can serve the second coming from this side of the veil very well by blending my presence with your own. Indeed the Christ has returned. Don't wait for me. Go look in the mirror! Many of you served me during my life as Jesus as I am now serving you. To the one who is asking, I am truly honored that you are so willing to receive my love. What stops that love from flowing when you look in the mirror? We both are serving the same love.

Question: So many are talking about a new Earth that is being designed to accommodate a higher vibration. What happens to those who are unable to match this new frequency?

Michael: Indeed. Creation offers a place for all of life, and there are places in creation where beings have chosen to experience life without love. For many of you, life without love is no life at all. Love will not force its presence into any aspect of creation, but it can be forced out. Love is the birthright and gift of every soul, but it is also a choice.

Many of you are beginning to experience, in this lifetime, the presence of an unconditional love. Its presence has made a profound impact on your life. Indeed, many of you discovered a new passion for living, inspiring you to use your creative abilities in a way that felt both awkward and empowering. The joy you now experience has changed the vibratory frequency of your own physical and non-physical bodies. None of you can truly say this new-found love made its way into your life without any resistance. In fact many of you would be so honest to say allowing this love into your life was the most challenging experience you've ever had as a human being.

Love has one condition, it cannot be contained and you call this new arena the new Earth. Self love has found a home in this new environment. This is not meant to ex-clude anyone, there is a place in creation for every vibration or choice.

It continues to be our joy to serve each and every one of you. To remind you that you may create for yourself any experience you desire. It simply asks of you to place your attention inward. Breathe in the life YOU want to feel with every breath you take and observe how your story, over time, begins to accept your newfound freedom. It all begins with your next breath!

Chapter Twelve

Questions and Answers • Part Two

Question: Now that 9/9/09 has come and gone, can you tell us when the next big portal will arrive? There also is channeled information about 2012 that suggests the magnetic poles on Earth will shift, can you share your perspective?

Yeshua: Indeed! We invite you to step back for a moment from all the energy that surrounds these cosmic events and simply observe all the reactions you are feeling. In this moment, the choices you are making have the potential for giving birth to any number of future events. The process of becoming conscious of your own creative abilities opens portals in your own life on a daily basis.

Individually, whenever you embrace life outside the story of your past, you create a profound impact on the currents of reality that support all of your choices. Life must yield to your new choice that is now willing to trust in your own heart's desires. The impact of such a choice isn't confined to your life, it begins to move into an expanded or collective version of itself. Over the last 20-30 years, many like yourself wanted to experience a new type of freedom that would allow you to enjoy your life with passion and wonder. Many choose to experiment with a number of healing modalities, and spiritual teachings, all designed to help break the codes of your past.

These cosmic events reflect the impact of those choices and now represent an expanded version of the changes each of you made individually. If you look at these events as something that is happening to you, outside of yourself, then you miss the opportunity to take ownership of your own creative abilities. So many of you wait for these moments on your calendar to give yourself permission to feel your own co-creative process. We want you to under-stand that for any of these cosmic events to exist at all, each of you, individually and now collectively must first give birth to the energy that supports them. The energy of 9/9/09 was created in your past and is now being celebrated and integrated as a collective experience. As an expanded version of your original intention, it has a more dynamic presence, but each of you have your name written on these events.

Take a deep breath and observe the energies that surround this event. Yes, celebrate them as an opportunity to now share with your human family what you created for yourself many years ago. Your human mind is already circling on your calendar the next portal that it believes will finally bring you the change you desire. Enjoy the life you are creating in this moment by being in the moment, which indeed is changing everything.

In regards to the shifting poles, this lifetime is very unique and represents the end of a particular cycle in creation. This cycle would have imploded upon itself if an expanded version of life wasn't honored. We want to remind you that none of you had to wait for this lifetime to ascend from your limitations, the opportunity also existed in your previous incarnations. There is nothing like the end of a cycle however to motivate your desires!

The reality of the poles shifting reflected a very real potential if humanity choose to resist the internal changes. Some would argue that this resistance still exists and in many ways we would agree. We now perceive a major shift in the pole that exists between your heart and your human mind. That indeed is reversing and creating a lot of challenges in your life. The external shift reflected a choice that would have been made for you if your human family chose not to make it for themselves. Gaia is now cooperating with this new internal shift, one that gives your human mind the vacation it deserves which in turn opens your life to receiving what your heart desires. Be patient, breathe in all of the support for your heart's desires on a moment-by-moment basis and watch the beauty of your own consciousness unfold.

Question: After Obama was elected there were a lot of expectations that he would represent a new kind of government. Instead, it seems like we have a system that has put future generations at risk by borrowing billions of dollars. What's the deal?

Yeshua: The real deal rests within each one of you. Are you now willing to take full responsibility for your own creations? Your government must follow the state of consciousness you choose to embody. There existed a choice within your government to simply cut off those that could not adapt, adjust or embrace the ways of your new administration. Compassion, however, prevailed by offering a lifejacket to those that have been denied the opportunity to work within this new way of perceiving life. Some would make the case that Obama's character has been tarnished because he refused to stand up to his own principals and yet those principals are not black and white. Every human being is entitled to have the opportunity to learn to work with the new energies that many of you have introduced. Our concern is not with your future generation but with your current one. Many rely and depend on a corrupt system that has denied humanity free access to all the benefits life has to offer. The role of the dictator is slowly ending, no matter what system it plays within.

Question: I am still confused by all this channeling business. Does Robert leave his body when Michael or Yeshua are speaking? If he doesn't, how do any of us know if these words are true?

Michael: We understand your concern. Robert also faced the same issue and believed for many years that he could best serve our message by removing himself from the relationship. Initially, he found it very frustrating every time he attempted to leave his body we would follow him. We have no interest in taking over anyone's body. We offer to blend or merge our presence out of mutual respect. If you want an authentic, unfiltered version of our truth, we suggest you drop all of your beliefs about yourself and experience the freedom that life has to offer. For now, we accept the distortions involved with all of our conditioned human companions.

Question: You often say that our divinity is within us and then go on to say that until we learn to receive, our divinity exists outside of us. Can you please elaborate, thank you.

Michael: Indeed! All of life is supported by the presence of Spirit. At the very core of your soul exists your divinity. Your divinity will not force itself upon you. If your mind insists on being in the drivers seat of your life, your divinity will not oppose that choice. Your divinity is all about giving life the freedom to choose for itself. Our teachings serve to encourage your mind to become a partner with your divinity by teaching it the art of being in receivership. Your divinity lives within your soul as an eternal partner. When your mind chooses to operate outside of this relationship, your divinity appears to be outside of you from your mind's perspective.

You, soul, are here on Earth to experience the joy of living inside your own creations. It asks of you to choose for yourself how you would want life to serve you. Once you become clear about that choice, your mind will stop trying to control your life and begin to serve your divine presence as a partner. It is but the beginning of a beautiful dance each of you are creating in your life.

Question: I find myself wanting to spend less time around other people and more time by myself with nature. It feels like a kind of self preservation, can you share your insights.

Yeshua: Indeed! We invite you to go deep within the forest that surrounds you. As you are walking between the trees, how does it feel? Most of you will share with us that you feel at peace, very content and deeply respected by nature. There is an exchange happening between the trees and you energetically that humanity is just beginning to learn. The trees share their presence with each other by maintaining a vertical connection with the source of life. Trees never vary from this relationship, and they offer a profound teaching to all of you by their example.

You have become very sensitive to energies that exist all around you. When you place your body within the sea of humanity, the energies run horizontally. This exchange is very debilitating, you have practiced shielding yourself from the onslaught of these unfulfilled desires. Shields, cutting cords and reflecting back energies are all vital tools in the process of creating a foundation, reclaiming your own sovereignty. Like many others, you practiced these tools because they serve your sense of wellbeing but they also filter your connection with Spirit.

The tree loves being a tree! It enjoys being a tree and can't imagine living anywhere else but here on Earth. It is now time for each of you to also claim this feeling even if your mind presents evidence to the contrary. Life wants to serve you! You will experience this truth when you consistently breathe in your heart's desires. The art of being in receivership asks of you to have an unfiltered relationship with life. You'll discover these horizontal energies will just pass through you. Put it to the test, go visit your local community, walk about town while breathing life in. Claim this freedom for yourself and notice now what your heart desires and then act on it. Thank you for your question for it is on the minds of many others.

Question: I've been on this ascension path for many years, and although I agree with many of the concepts, like being in the moment, I still find it impossible to quiet my mind. I would love to experience the joy and wonder you speak of, what am I doing wrong?

Yeshua: In my life as Jesus, I too discovered that the mind is very resistant to change, especially when the change we are talking about involves giving up control of our lives. This is no easy task, very few people are willing to face the same frustrations, challenges, and anxieties you have experienced. That is why Michael and I and many others honor your choice. It would be far easier to simply ignore your passion for a more fulfilling life. It would be much easier if you would just accept the life that society expects from you, living up to the expectations others have created for you. Your freedom won't be given to you by anyone else. Your human mind won't resign its position as the CEO of your life. But over time, with practice you will experience the joy and wonder many speak of. You have already discovered your freedom escapes you when you try really hard to achieve it. It comes to you when you surrender all the effort and reduce your life to one breath at a time. One breath, simply breathing in your heart's desires. Your heart hasn't forgotten what joy feels like. One breath at a time puts the human mind in service to your soul. I, Yeshua, can promise you that if you devote yourself to placing your attention on breathing life in on a regular basis, your life will indeed change. Yes, the mind will insist that there are more important things to do. It will become bored, restless with this whole notion that you don't need it to direct your life for you. It will also, over time, experience the benefits from not feeling responsible for your life and will begin to relish serving your heart. For behind all these control issues, your human mind, like everything else in life, just wants to be respected, honored, and loved!

Question: Over 20 years ago, I left my day job with a passion for serving others. I studied a variety of holistic healing modalities and slowly built an alternative practice. Like a lot of other women, I felt I had the capacity to give to others what they were lacking. My business grew over the years but during the last two years, I started to feel disillusioned. I keep seeing the same people, with the same issues who seem to just want me to pamper them on many levels.

171

I've become bitter, resentful and this of course has impacted my business. I am now once again looking for that secure day job to support myself. I want to continue to serve, but I seem to have lost the passion and enthusiasm that inspired me 20 years ago. Your comments and insights would be greatly appreciated.

Michael: We want to thank you for being so honest. The role of a healer, like everything else on Earth, is shifting. For a very long time, your human family has been under the domain of a mind that feels it doesn't need to have a conscious relationship with its own creator - consciousness. It lacks the tools or resources to embody its own healing abilities by separating itself from the source of all healing.

It has been the role of the healer to act as a bridge between Spirit and those in need of healing. That role is now changing, and it is now no longer appropriate, no matter your gender, to act as the source for others to rely on. We celebrate your shift, even though it might appear that you have somehow failed in your profession. To the contrary, you can now serve others in a way that doesn't leave you feeling depleted, exhausted, or disrespected. This will ask of you to also look at the role you play as the Mother. We would say this is one of the more challenging shifts for any woman to embrace. We won't mince words with you, you are being summoned by the Priestess to now serve life from a more self empowered perspective. We will speak more about this in another session, but the Priestess is here to teach. She doesn't use nurturing as a healing tool, she is more interested in cutting through the illusions that deny yourself your own magnificence. The new healer becomes the Priestess embodied, she embraces a type of spiritual selfishness that honors the self as being sacred. You are now being asked to stop denying yourself the pleasures of life. It is time to look at what YOU desire before sharing those gifts with others.

Once you claim the sacredness of your own life, what you share can be the overflow of what you first give to yourself. If you allow it, your mind can be relieved of all of its responsibilities by accepting its new role. The mind now serves the energy or presence of your new consciousness. It is a relationship that signals the end of the age of the mind that insisted that life serve its own agenda outside its relationship with consciousness. Embrace this opportunity and we can see you serving yourself and others with a renewed sense of passion and wonder.

It is our joy to serve our human family. We now have access to your physical reality in a way that reunites your soul with the presence of many galactic families. It continues to be our joy to witness the sovereign creator unfold it's wings with integrity, compassion and love.

Chapter Thirteen

Riding a Stallion

Our devotion to serving you is infinite. We have the advantage of knowing the true nature of your soul when you are not engaged in breaking the codes of duality. Prior to your incarnation, we promised to serve you in any way you would allow us, by reminding you that you are not the conditions you have inherited. Your true nature has already ascended. By that, we mean you have already experienced your mind being of service to your heart. In that relationship you have already claimed your soul to be united within you. Only those who have tasted the fruits of a united consciousness could enter into this web of confusion to be the new teachers. We use that term to describe the unlimited expression of your love for yourself. Your devotion to your soul family has you entering into a vast array of realities. It might appear to be a great sacrifice on your part to volunteer to forget your true nature by adapting to the collective consciousness at hand. You would taste the pain and suffering of that consciousness knowing that it takes but a glimmer of love to reawaken your authentic self. There is great joy in planting seeds of love within the barren landscapes of fear. Many of you have already experienced your heart awakening from its deep sleep, while others have just begun this journey. It is through the heart that we are able to reconnect with each of you. Our agreement is to remind you that your past does not define the magnificent being we know you to be. As you grow to recognize that for yourself, you also begin to reveal the nature of Christ consciousness fully embodied as a human being.

Each of you reading these words has experienced the stirring in your heart. You are questioning your reality, the roles you are playing in your personal relationships, in your jobs, and within yourself. Our service to you is to inspire you to heal your inner conflict and to discover a love for yourself that is not dependent on being loved by someone else first. We are encouraging each of you not to take our words at face value. We have no interest in providing more concepts for your mind to consider. The value of our teaching is directly related to the enhancement of your day-to-day reality. You must be willing to put yourself in experiences that will challenge the dualistic nature of your inherited beliefs, shifting the very nature of your perceptions which have relied on your mind. Your family and friends will pull on you to remain attached to continue playing the victim game. You did not come here, soul, to offer an improved version of victimhood. You did not descend from the stars to introduce a fully awakened, empowered victim. You volunteered to embody Spirit as a living example for all of life to witness.

In our relationship with you, we too have come to a crossroad. Our words can inspire you, but they cannot give you the experience that your heart yearns to feel. The choice to physically embody your authentic nature has only been experienced by a few humans. There are millions of you now contemplating this leap. The describer—your mind—continues to serve you by trying to create a safe passage for you. It is not your mind's responsibility to make this leap for you. It cannot give you the details of a life that is free of duality until you, soul, free yourself.

Within the perception of your heart, we now invite you to leave behind the pain and sorrow of your past and feel the presence of Spirit whirling in and around every cell of your body. We see before each of you a new opportunity existing in a vast open prairie. This symbolizes the openness to expand upon more of who you are, and we celebrate that. It is a grand prairie. Standing next to you is a horse that has served you for most of your life. This horse looks weary, bored, and disillusioned. Its back is bowed, and its head almost touches the ground. A rope is tied to its neck and is attached to a center pole guiding its walk around a well trodden path. There is very little joy left in this horse, but its sense of duty and devotion has it walking in circles over and over again. You climb onto this horse, and we see how comfortable and complacent you have become riding this companion. You have also given this horse a name that we now come to remind you. You call it Denial! Surrounding this well traveled path is a fence, and sitting on the fence is your past. Your family, friends, husbands and wives, coworkers, and 98% of humanity. It is a grand gathering to witness such a downtrodden event. The discussions on this fence generate much sympathy for numerous failings and grand scheming for achieving that elusive contentment. You invite us to meet this horse, sharing that, although the ride can be boring, it is safe and comfortable. You have said to us that if you continue looking directly in front of you, you are never sidetracked by all the diversions and distractions of life. We smile, but politely decline.

You show us that on occasion you have jumped off this horse, sat on the outlying fence, and gazed at the vast prairie behind you. Others have suggested that you are wasting your time daydreaming, encouraging you to put your efforts into things that are real. We invite you to look at us eye to eye and ask: "Why are you riding this horse called Denial, dear soul?" You look at us a little puzzled and invite us to go back in time and remember the grand celebration just prior to leaving the Kingdom. Indeed, we see a grand celebration taking place. You have just received the ultimate gift from God/Goddess. They bestowed all of their creative abilities to you that all may embody a love that is uncontained.

We see you and many others preparing to leave the Kingdom while sitting on the back of a grand stallion. These horses are bursting with fire pouncing their hooves with excitement for this new adventure. The stallions prance about, filling the air with expectation and wonder. Their heads are held high and their eyes are blazing with determination and trust. Fire is bursting from their nostrils as they prepare themselves to journey into the unknown. The excitement is building and it is overwhelming. Suddenly there is a resounding, unified chant—NOW! In that moment, these stallions burst forward. Your arms are spread like an eagle over your head. With your eyes closed, you blissfully gallop to the very edge of the Kingdom exploding into the vastness of the void itself.

We take a deep breath. Yes, what a magnificent story. It reminds us why it is that we have chosen to serve you. Looking at this horse called Denial, we wonder why you and humanity would choose such a horse now that you reside on the other side of the Kingdom. The passion to discover a love uncontained has faced many challenges. You have questioned many aspects of yourself, including the wisdom to trust in a passion that brought you to this new reality. What a grand, grand story! We saw your adventures as you discovered and created new star systems. We see the yearning in your heart to return home to experience the familiar relationship with a love that came directly from God/Goddess, your original Mother and Father. We see your turmoil in accepting the gift to be sovereign and complete within yourself. We see humanity playing out these deep-seeded feelings, day after day.

Indeed, your galactic history has been grand! Your wisdom to honestly examine and embrace your own reflection is also a part of your past here on earth. There is something new however stirring within your heart. When you have turned and looked out into that vast landscape, that open prairie of new opportunities, you have noticed that there also exists another horse. It raises its body off the ground while standing on its back legs and sings its song of freedom. Pouncing the ground it turns its head and looks directly into your eyes. "You know me, soul. I am a Stallion!"

With your knees feeling a little weak, you proclaim, "Yes, I know you!" A part of you feels pulled to return to the safety of the horse called Denial. That horse reminds you of all the pain and turmoil, all the disappointment, frustration, and anger this stallion has brought you. You ponder this while feeling a passion within this stallion that begins to stir your curiosity.

Suddenly you jump off the fence and begin to walk towards this stallion. All of those still sitting on the fence begin to shout at you, "It's not safe to venture out into that open prairie!" You hesitate for a moment and begin to listen to their fears when it strikes you that you have heard these same concerns your whole life. You face the stallion again and with each step you begin to feel more alive as if waking up from a long sleep. Excitement begins to brew as your walking quickly turns to running. The voices of those still sitting on the fence begin to fade. You notice the smell of the grass in this prairie is intensely sweet. The air feels crisp and alive while the sun seems to be massaging your heart. You begin to pick up speed, running now with complete abandon, feeling layers of decaying energy sliding off your body.

Finally you reach this stallion. It indeed is a most beautiful and powerful horse. As it turns to look at you, gazing with much affection and admiration as it pounds the earth with its hoof and proclaims, "Ride me!" You are shocked by your response. Without any hesitation, you jump on its back, clinging to its mane while this stallion bursts into a full gallop. It takes your breath away as you wrap your arms around its neck and it turns to you and says, "Relax, let her presence ride with me."

Slowly you loosen your grip, relax your arms, and begin to feel your heart bursting with joy. Your arms begin to rise above your head, you close your eyes as this stallion begins to soar across the plains of this prairie. Wave upon wave of bliss and ecstasy ripple throughout your entire body. With tears flowing in all directions you shout for all of life to hear—"I am Home! Finally I am Home—free at last!"

The stallion stops, and you open your eyes expecting to find yourself back in the embracement of the Kingdom, but you find that you are still on this open prairie. "How can this be?" This energy you now feel is what your soul has been searching for since you left the Kingdom. It is home! How could it be here with this stallion in this open prairie?

Your eyes are now wide open, and you begin to notice in the distance a herd of stallions with riders galloping towards you. Memories of grand galactic confrontations begin to surface. Your stallion again turns to you and reminds you to relax and let her presence support this ride. As this herd gets closer, you notice the faces of these strangers appear to be smiling and rejoicing at your arrival. Could it be? Your horse turns to look at you as more tears begin to flow. "Michael? My entire soul family—you are here?" You are suddenly surrounded by a wave of congratulations, laughter, and joy. Archangel Michael steps off his horse and deeply bows before you. "It is so good to see you again! We thought we lost you while you were riding that other horse of yours." Everyone laughs, slapping you on the back while embracing you.

You turn to Michael and ask, "Can I ride this stallion and still be on earth?"

Michael's eyes glimmer, "Indeed, and we can ride with you!"

You ask, "Must we be separate from each other, for I cannot bear the pain any longer?"

Michael puts his hand on your shoulder. "No longer must you deny yourself the fruits of your desires. You have discovered while playing human the solution to your pain. You have allowed your male and female nature to ride together. And do not bliss and passion make for a delicious ride?"

You gaze at this magnificent archangel, "Yes, indeed they do my friend!"

A Life of Service

Our companion (Robert) discovered us while riding upon these plains within his own imagination, bringing that experience into his day-to-day reality. Many of you have placed your feet upon this open prairie, only to be discouraged by the many voices within yourself and in your culture. Most of you are attempting to live your life while straddling both realities. We will say it again—you did not come here to discover an improved version of duality. You are here to discover a solution to the polarized relationship within yourself. We often hear, "What is the most accelerated path to embodying our ascended state of consciousness as a human being?" We would suggest a life that is supported by the Heart and Mind of Creation freely expressing itself in unlimited, self-fulfilling experiences. Love will not be content being contained. Your life will serve the solution you discover while riding this stallion. A life of service is a very potent way of living. In this new relationship, it does not ask of you to sacrifice your personal well-being, to compromise your value, or to negotiate your joy. It does not require that you perfect the healing of your inner conflicts. Being of service is serving your own self-fulfillment. It is loving yourself by sharing the many gifts you already embody.

Many of you are just beginning to contemplate if there is a life outside this corral. We are here to serve the human that desires to be free and to stop relying on this horse you call Denial. We cannot twist your arm to convince you that this is in your best interest. We can inspire you to experience the presence of a sovereign heart that chooses a way of life without compromising its worth.

Each of you carries the mantle of Christ consciousness within you. You have discovered that there is very little support for such a consciousness in a reality that is divided within itself. You have attempted to break the chains of duality by relying on your mind to force yourself free. Your mind is waiting for the ride of your life. This stallion represents a life that unites your mind, body, and soul with the Heart and Mind of Creation/Spirit. Spirit will not force you to change. It invites each of you to choose for yourself. Your new freedom has nothing to do with adapting to the collective consciousness of humanity. For humanity will continue to insist that if you do not adapt, you will not survive. Lying outside that corral of fear is an unlimited expression of love. In that open prairie, you become reunited with your soul family reawakening the memory of your true self and reigniting your desire to embody Christ consciousness—your authentic self!

There is a grand celebration waiting for each of you. As our words for this book come to an end, it is also an invitation for a new beginning. The next chapter is now your life. How it will unfold will be your choice. Together, we may serve this polarized reality. You are the new teachers who have come riding upon this earth on grand stallions which are supported by Spirit. Now is the time to choose a life that is not clouded by your doubts and fears. Now is the time to trust that your feelings are your best barometer. Is there a storm looming in your horizon or will you allow the clouds to pass and enjoy the fruits of a clear mind and an open heart that have fallen in love with each other? Your life will demonstrate that Spirit will freely come to you. It only asks that you put Denial in the stable and give it the rest it deserves. It is safe to reveal your gifts, trust your passions, and let life support your new creations. There is a grand family reunion waiting for each of you.

It is time to once again ride this magnificent stallion that gallops within the heart of Spirit. It is time to ride your new passions with a renewed sense of joy and enthusiasm. It is time for you to love yourself in all the ways that you had hoped others would do for you. It is time to allow an undiluted version of yourself to be present and joyfully engaged with life. It is time to acknowledge your fears, placing yourself in experiences that serve to heal your guilt. This is your time to become what you have yearned to feel your whole life. It is your time to accept a new relationship that is just now unfolding within you, knowing that even in its infancy, its reflection inspires and motivates humanity to question a life that lacks joy.

Your true identity is love itself. It is not a burden. It is a gift! If you allow it, we now ride by your side each day, supporting your gift, your service that is supported by your love. Now is that time to live life knowing that 'your' life offers the very solution to humanity's troubled mind. You are here to offer tangible evidence that the Heart and Mind of Creation are real. How many ways are you willing to see that presence in yourself reflected back for all of life to see? Sharing the embodied presence of self-love makes self-fulfillment complete. It is time to bring your presence full circle. How may we now serve you, dear soul?

APPENDIX A

Spirit Comes to You / Exercise

This is a beautiful practice that encourages us to feel the perfection of who we are in this moment. We tend to spend so much of our lives pursuing personal agendas seeking to achieve what we believe we lack within ourselves. Opening your life to the feeling that Spirit truly does come to YOU will dramatically change your priorities, perspectives, and beliefs about yourself.

Give yourself at least 30 minutes of undisturbed time to fully experience this practice. Find a place in your home or outside that feels comfortable and inviting to you. Spend a few minutes appreciating your life while you breathe in that feeling with each breath. Now imagine that physical creation all around you is radiating the energy of vitality, passion, and well-being. Imagine that physical reality is overflowing with a feeling of being self-fulfilled and it freely shares this love with ALL. Let yourself go deeply into how it might feel for you to simply be in receivership of this continuous flow of energy that is radiating all around you in everything you see, touch, hear, and feel. Let it come into the top of your head, the bottom of your feet, the front, back, and sides of your body. For the next 30 minutes, the most important task for you to accomplish is to simply love yourself so deeply that you allow the love that is all around you to be shared with you. If your mind becomes bored with this love wash, thinking of more important projects and activities for you to engage in, gently bring your attention back to how it feels to be in this new receivership of love.

Try practicing this new relationship with life for several days. It is not uncommon not to feel anything, initially. You will need to be patient with yourself as you slowly break down the resistance of loving yourself in this way. The moment you taste the ecstatic reunion with Spirit/Love, you will discover that, no matter where you are, Spirit comes to you, if you allow it. You will experience this energy flowing into you as a reflection of your self-fulfillment. Reality will mirror back to you your love affair with you!

This practice becomes far more than just another spiritual exercise. It becomes a way of life that frees you from a polarized reality.

APPENDIX B

Cutting the Connections / Exercise

A polarized, dualistic reality lives by its own set of rules; opposition and confrontation, pushing and pulling agendas, extracting energy to gain dominance. These tend to overwhelm our ability to cooperate, to trust and to freely share love. Learning to be in receivership changes our interactions with all of life. We learn to rely on this new connection within ourselves and see it reflected back to us. We also develop a sensitivity to energies that are a result of feeling disconnected from self-love. You can feel these in your body running horizontally—chakra to chakra. This dualistic relationship is also referred to as 'cording.' Cording is the energetic byproduct of indirect communication, manipulation, and control. If you are feeling it is time for you to choose a non-dualistic approach to life, the following exercise can serve your personal awareness. Personal relationships that invite a sharing between two or more self-fulfilled individuals rely on open communication, trust, and honesty.

Appendix B

In this exercise, we again put to practice our new
sense of self-love by choosing not to engage in these horizontal connections. This might feel awkward at first as you
get in touch with how all of us have learned to sacrifice our
personal well-being to please others. This practice will reinforce your willingness to simply share the overflow of
love that you have first given to yourself. You can celebrate
releasing guilt and shame from your life as you embrace
this new understanding of love.

To disconnect these energetic cords between people,
start by imagining that your body is supported by a vertical
relationship with life. Universal love responds to your love
for yourself flowing into the top of your head. Coming up
from the center of the earth is another stream of love that
flows into your feet or the base of your spine. Let yourself
feel these energies from above and below supporting you
without any agenda.

Now imagine anyone you would like to change your
relationship with; perhaps a family member, your mother or
father, children, husband or wife, co-workers, friends, past
or current lovers. They do not need to be physically present. Simply imagine this person standing in front of you
and communicate with them that you would like to offer a
new relationship. The love you now want to share with oth-

191

ers comes from taking responsibility for receiving that for ourselves rather than from each other. Imagine that between each of your chakras is a line of energy that connects you with this person. With each chakra, cut this connection with your tool of choice. Some prefer scissors, others prefer swords or even chain saws to disconnect from this corded relationship. When you have finished, take a moment to notice if it was more difficult disconnecting from certain chakras? You might need to go back several times to reinforce your intention. Did you also notice a sense of relief and peace within yourself? At the end of each session, make sure your vertical connection feels intact and imagine making that connection for the person you have just decorded from. With practice, you can disconnect yourself from these horizontal relationships simply by imagining a mirror in front of your body reflecting back what is attempting to be projected into your body.

It is not uncommon for those you have disconnected from to contact you with an openness to discuss unresolved issues. They also might feel very betrayed by your new sense of freedom. Explain to them how self-love is changing all of your relationships.

APPENDIX C

Creating a New PhotoAlbum / Exercise

The Family of Michael will often refer to our personal history as a photo album of our soul's journey since we have left the kingdom. It is an honored story that is based on our perceptions of feeling separate from home. That separation created duality. This family now invites us to experience a new potential by creating a new photo album. Each of us face some new challenges to make this perception real.

One of those challenges is the relationship we have with our personality or human mind. It serves us very well as our photographer and guardian of our personal history. However it is reluctant to allow any new experiences that might invite potential harm to our heart. The personality sees all those old pictures as valid evidence that change can be harmful to our well-being, believing that the world we live in is not safe.

The Teachings of Michael offer another perception for us to play with. Michael invites us to experience in our day-to-day reality, what he calls, joy dates. In this exercise, you can experience first hand tangible evidence of your own conscious ability to create rewarding and uplifting experiences for yourself.

Imagine any experience, perhaps something from your childhood, that feels to you like it just might be a lot of fun. It would serve you to keep a journal of these imagined possibilities for future reference. Here are just a few ideas to help you get started.

* Spending time alone in nature
* Reading a book in a park or perhaps by a fireplace
* Treating yourself to an afternoon cup of tea and chocolate

Or perhaps something a little more adventuresome:
* Dressing up, going out in public and role playing another personality
* Dancing naked under the moonlight or rain
* Listen to an entire CD with your full attention B no interruptions
* Writing a book

Let your imagination really play with these joy dates. Put it on your calendar, and give it the same devotion you give to brushing your teeth. At the end of each joy date, invite your personality to photograph this new experience and imagine it being placed in a new photo album. The personality will honor it as long as it was a tangible experience, but it will still need more fulfilling pictures to change its devotion to your new photo album. Over time and with practice, it will stop acting as your guardian, protecting a well-documented story of a painful history. By engaging in joy dates, you give yourself new and uplifting experiences. These will reassure the personality over time that the world is indeed a safe place to live.

Other Books by Robert Theiss

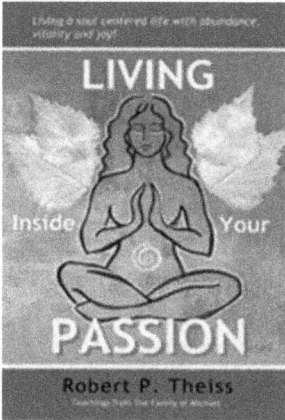

Living Inside your Passion

All of humanity is beginning to experience a very intense transition from relying on a conditioned identity that feels disconnected from love. This dramatic shift is impacting every aspect of our personal and global affairs. It is inviting us to reclaim our creative abilities by jumping into the river of our passions, awakening our heart felt desires to flow with the ongoing current of creation.

In his second book, Robert Theiss openly shares his relationship with The Family of Michael. They offer an uplifting and refreshing perspective that has inspired thousands worldwide to reclaim the true nature of the soul with compassion, integrity and joy.

Living Inside Your Passion

Paperback / ISBN: 978-0-578-00664-2

156 pages / $14.95

Published by Ancient Wings®

www.ingramcontent.com/pod-product-compliance
Lightning Source LLC
LaVergne TN
LVHW011227080426
835509LV00005B/364